# Longing for
# H O M E

## A JOURNEY THROUGH
## THE PSALMS OF ASCENT

# J. STEPHEN YUILLE

Shepherd Press
Wapwallopen, Pennsylvania

*Longing for Home*
© 2015 by James Stephen Yuille

Published by Shepherd Press
P.O. Box 24
Wapwallopen, Pennsylvania 18660

Unless otherwise noted, all Scripture citations are from The Holy Bible, English Standard Version, copyright 2001 by Crossway, a publishing ministry of Good News Publishers.

Typesetting by Lakeside Design Plus
Cover Design by Tobias' Outerwear for Books

First Printing, 2015
Printed in the United States of America

BP 22 21 20 19 18 17 16 15
14 13 12 11 10 9 8 7 6 5 4 3 2 1

---------------------------------------------

Library of Congress Cataloging-in-Publication Data

Yuille, J. Stephen, 1968-
 Longing for home : a journey through the Psalms of ascent / J. Stephen Yuille.
    pages cm
 Includes bibliographical references.
 ISBN 978-1-63342-097-7 (print book : alk. paper)—ISBN 978-1-63342-098-4 (epub ebook)—ISBN 978-1-63342-099-1 (kindle ebook)  1.  Bible. Psalms, CXX-CXXXIV—Meditations.  I. Title.
 BS1445.S6Y85 2015
 223'.2077—dc23
                                 2015015233

eBooks: www.shepherdpress.com/ebooks

*In memory of*
*Mikayla Jayne Dent*
*December 11–18, 2004*

Dear Daniel —
Merry Christmas with
love in Jesus and profound
appreciation for your friend-
ship and fellowship in
Christ's Kingdom work —
Tedd and Margy
2 Peter 1:3, 4

# Contents

# Preface

Some feelings are difficult to put into words. Occasionally, I experience a sudden sense of familiarity, which creates a deep longing that I can neither express nor fulfill. It happens in front of a roaring fire around Christmas time, or on a cool autumn afternoon as the sun nears the end of its descent. It occurs when I see gray skies and barren hills, or I hear certain strains of music, or I smell freshly cut grass on a warm summer evening. It begins to stir as I drive past my childhood home or recall childhood friends. In each of these instances, I sense something familiar yet missing.

On a far greater level, all of us experience what C. S. Lewis calls "life-long nostalgia."[1] It stems from our inexpressible longing to be reunited with something in the universe from which we feel isolated—something familiar yet missing. This *something* is God, of course. He created us in his image, so that we might find our rest and center in him. But we broke away from him, and we have lived with the isolation ever since.

In 2012, an elderly woman in the city of Borja, Spain, realized that a familiar fresco painted on one of the church walls was looking a little faded. The fresco, *Ecce Homo*, was a rendition of Christ standing trial before Pontius Pilate.[2] The woman took it upon herself to attempt a restoration of the nearly century-old piece of art. The result was disastrous. According to one report, she turned the painting into something resembling a "bloated hedgehog."[3] Sadly, that's us. Sin has marred us beyond recognition. As a result of this defacing, we've lost the life of God and the enjoyment of God, and this isolation has led to our "life-long nostalgia."

But the story doesn't end here. Mercifully, the Son of God has drawn near to us in the incarnation. He who made all things was carried in the womb of a woman, and he who upholds all things was held in the arms of a woman. He clothed himself with our humanity—body and soul. He came so close as to experience life in a fallen world, bear our sin and shame, and taste death for us. He was bruised, that we might be healed; humiliated, that we might be exalted; condemned, that we might be justified. At that moment of utter darkness and forsakenness upon the cross, he purchased the enjoyment of God for us—restoration and reconciliation. His forgiveness now supersedes our sinfulness, his merit eclipses our guilt, and his righteousness hides our vileness. His "abundant mercy" blots out our multitude of "transgressions" (Psalm 51:1).

By virtue of our union with Christ, we draw near to God and find in him all we could ever want: an eternal and spiritual good, suitable to our every need. Our knowledge of this God diffuses into our soul a satisfying peace in this life and a tantalizing taste of what awaits us in glory. Having returned to our center, we live in anticipation of the *beatific* vision—the day we will see God (Matthew 5:8). In one sense, we see him right now through the eyes of faith, but that's nothing in comparison to what's coming. At present, we see God's perfections in their effects, namely his works of creation, providence, and redemption; but in the future, we will see *him* perfectly.

We will be like Christ and therefore able to commune with God to the fullest capacities of our souls. There will be nothing to obscure, confound, or hinder our enjoyment of him. Our knowledge of God will be full and perfect, constant and complete, resulting in hitherto unknown delight as we rest fully and finally in him. Until then, we're on a journey fraught with joys and sorrows, pleasant valleys and perilous mountains, encouraging gains and crippling losses—a journey marked by rejoicing, grieving, searching, wondering, and longing.

And that brings us to this book, *Longing for Home: A Journey through the Psalms of Ascent*. We are not exactly sure why these fifteen psalms—chapters 120–134—are called the Psalms of Ascent. One of the more plausible explanations for the description *ascent* (or *degree*) is that the Israelites sang this collection of psalms as they traveled (ascended) to the city of Jerusalem to celebrate one of their annual festivals, which we read about in Deuteronomy 16:16.

A unique feature of the psalms in general is that they express the whole range of human emotions. John Calvin refers to them as "an anatomy of all the parts of the soul, for there is not an emotion of which any one can be conscious that is not here represented as in a mirror."[4] What is true of the Book of Psalms in general is true of the Psalms of Ascent in particular. In short, they're a catalogue of human experience. They take us on a journey through life's many ups and downs. In so doing, they shape our perspectives, regulate our feelings, and inform our judgments. They guide us into the path of God-glorifying desires, God-magnifying emotions, and God-honoring thoughts. They equip us to pray in faith, as they beckon us to fix our eyes heavenward.

Whenever we feel besieged on our journey, we tend to turn to whatever we think can help us—another program, another seminar, another counselor. Far too often, however, we neglect the help God has given us—the Book of Psalms, and the Psalms of Ascent, in particular. In them, we connect with people who've traveled the very road we're traveling. If we listen carefully, they teach us how to look to God in every circumstance of life, and they demonstrate how this shift in our perspective strengthens our faith and enlarges our hope.

I trust this pastoral emphasis will become apparent as you make your way through this book, and I pray God will bless it to your spiritual comfort and his eternal glory.

Deus pro nobis

# Introduction

For many Ontarians, Spring Break (or March Break, as it's called north of the border) is one of the most significant weeks on the calendar. After three or four months of enduring short days, freezing temperatures, and blinding blizzards, Ontarians rush south to thaw in the sunshine. When we lived in Ontario, we occasionally joined our fellow snowbirds in the annual trek and headed out to Orlando, Florida.

Before setting off, we dutifully visited CAA (the Canadian equivalent of AAA) to take advantage of one of their many services, *Travel Tips*. These *tips* included a map with highlighted route and step-by-step directions to get to Orlando from Toronto. The selected route was based on up-to-date reports concerning toll booths, road works, and speed traps (some state troopers love those Ontario license plates). Of course, these *tips* were extremely valuable as we navigated 1,200 miles of highway.

As we embark on this journey through the Psalms of Ascent, I want to provide four travel tips, which I think will prove useful as we navigate through these fifteen chapters.

## Travel Tip #1: Stay Focused on the Gospel

Isn't this stating the obvious? Yes, but sometimes we need to remind ourselves of the blatantly obvious. Why do I say that? Simply put, we're easily amused and distracted, and we often fill our lives with things that seem harmless but are detrimental if we don't keep them in their proper place. I'm thinking about things like tweeting, blogging, shopping, watching movies, playing sports, purchasing another gadget or gizmo . . . the list goes on and on. There's nothing wrong with any of these *things,* of course, unless we use them as substitutes for the *main* thing. Consider the following story:

> On Monday, Alice bought a parrot. It didn't talk, so the next day she returned to the pet store. "He needs a ladder," she was told. She bought a ladder, but another day passed and the parrot still didn't say a word. "How about a swing?", the clerk suggested. So Alice bought a swing; the next day, a mirror; the next day, a miniature plastic tree; the next day, a shiny parrot toy.
> On Sunday morning, Alice was standing outside the pet store when it opened. She had the parrot cage in her hand and tears in her eyes. Her parrot was dead. "Did it ever say a word?" the store owner asked. "Yes," Alice said through her sobs. "Right before he died, he looked at me and asked, 'Don't they sell any food at that pet store?'"[1]

When we try to fill our lives with anything but the main thing (the gospel), we're just like Alice's bird—starving in a cage crowded with pretty toys. When the gospel is no longer at the center, we soon feel the effects in every facet of our lives—from the home, to the church, to the workplace, and at all points in between. For this reason, we must constantly orient our lives around the gospel: the good news that God saves sinners from his wrath for his glory through Christ's substitutionary death.

We can't save ourselves. It's absurd to think otherwise. For a moment, let's imagine I own a famous painting, displayed proudly in my living room. One day, a dinner guest decides (for some inconceivable reason) to scribble all over it with a black marker. My painting is ruined. Perceiving my displeasure, my guest reaches for the magazine stand, grabs a catalogue from Cabela's, tears out a picture of the latest apparel in hunter orange, glues it to the painting, and assures me that the artwork is as good as new. What's my response? For starters, I question my guest's mental health. Then, I ridicule his feeble attempt to restore the painting. He can't fix it. It's ruined!

Likewise, we can't fix ourselves. There are no Band-Aid solutions because the problem runs too deep. Our sin touches every thought, shapes every desire, corrupts every word, and taints every deed. Because of our sin, we're "storing up wrath" for the day when God's righteous judgment will be revealed (Romans 2:5). This expression "storing up" means gradual accumulation. That is, God's wrath is like the water gathering behind a dam. It rises and rises until the dam bursts. That stored-up wrath awaits sinners.

But the good news is that God saves sinners. In Christ, God's wrath is turned away. God punished Christ, so that he might forgive us. God condemned Christ, so that he might justify us. In giving himself, Christ revealed the Father's love for us. In love, he climbed a shameful cross to bear our guilt and shame, pouring out his soul to death.

Christ declares, "Truly, I say to you, unless you turn and become like children, you will never enter the kingdom of heaven" (Matthew 18:3). When our children call for us in the middle of the night or climb into our lap to cuddle, when they cry for us after falling down, take our hand as they stumble over uneven ground, look to us for protection and direction, and call us *daddy* or *mommy,* do we realize what we're witnessing? The way into the kingdom!

Before God's holiness, we're humbled for our sinfulness. Recognizing our helplessness to save ourselves, we come to Christ in childlike dependence, and look to him alone to save us. Wonder of wonders! God receives us in Christ—his Beloved. He saves us so that we can enjoy the beauty of his glory. He saves us so that we can be satisfied in his incomprehensible greatness and goodness.

This glorious gospel is the *main* thing—our lives must revolve around this center. It's important to have a firm grasp on this idea as we journey through the Psalms of Ascent.

## Travel Tip #2: Stay Focused on the Kingdom

What does the kingdom have to do with the Psalms of Ascent? Much more than you might initially think. In John 5:39, Christ declares, "You search the Scriptures because you think that in them you have eternal life; and it is they that bear witness about me." Thomas Adams explains the significance of Christ's claim as follows: "[He is] the sum of the whole Bible, prophesied, typified, prefigured, exhibited, demonstrated, to be found in every leaf, almost in every line, the Scriptures being but as it were the swaddling bands of the child Jesus."[2] Today, it seems many people have forgotten that the central theme of the Old Testament is Christ. Jeremy Walker compares this trend to an imaginary art gallery, containing numerous portraits of just one man painted by just one artist.[3] The gallery has two main sections: the first is bright, clean, and tidy, and it receives plenty of visitors; but the second is dark, dirty, and messy, and it receives very few visitors. Why? Over time, some people began to suggest that the artist's early portraits weren't his best effort. Some of these people went so far as to imply that it wasn't the same man in the early portraits as in the later portraits. And so, most people stopped visiting the older section of the art gallery. Gradually, its rooms fell into disrepair because no one fixed the lights, cleaned the floors, or dusted the portraits. Now, very few people venture anywhere near this section of the gallery because they don't think it contains anything worth seeing. That's precisely how many Christians approach the Old Testament. Simply put, most don't think Christ is there, and the few who do venture in are no longer equipped to find him.

We must never lose sight of the fact that the Old Testament is about Christ—that the Scriptures are "the swaddling bands of the child Jesus." He fulfills its promises and prophecies, ceremonies and rituals, hopes and desires. At the outset of his ministry, Christ announced, "The time is fulfilled, and the kingdom of God is at hand" (Mark 1:15). Obviously, a fulfillment requires a promise.

So what promise was Christ talking about? He was declaring that the Old Testament expectation concerning the arrival of God's kingdom was fulfilled. In the days of the patriarchs, this kingdom was promised; in the days of the judges, it was prefigured; in the days of the kings, it was previewed; and in the days of the prophets, it was prophesied. That is to say, God's plan concerning his kingdom was progressively revealed throughout the Old Testament. At his first coming, Christ inaugurated this kingdom: "The time is fulfilled." At his second coming, he will consummate this kingdom. Between his two comings, he reigns as Mediator (1 Corinthians 15:23–26; Ephesians 1:22; Hebrews 10:12–13).

When we turn to the Old Testament, therefore, we interpret it not as an end in itself but in light of its ultimate end: Christ and his kingdom. This is also the way we approach the Psalms of Ascent. We view them through the lens of Christ and his mediatorial kingdom.

## Travel Tip #3: Stay Focused on the Glory

Paul declares, "For I consider that the sufferings of this present time are not worth comparing to the glory that is to be revealed to us" (Romans 8:18). The verb "consider" refers to a process of reasoning that leads to a conclusion. And so Paul puts present suffering on one side and future glory on the other side and uses his power of reasoning to compare the two.

What's his conclusion? Interestingly, he doesn't conclude that future glory is slightly greater than present suffering; nor does he conclude that future glory is twice as great as present suffering—or a hundred times or a thousand times greater than present suffering. He concludes, "The sufferings of this present time are not worth comparing to the glory that is to be revealed." Paul's focus on future glory gives him a perspective that enables him to endure present suffering. As Christians, we desperately need this kind of perspective.

In 1952, a young woman by the name of Florence Chadwick stepped off the beach at Catalina Island and into the water, determined to swim to the shore of mainland California. She had already achieved great heights as a long-distance swimmer, becoming the first woman to swim the English Channel both ways. The weather was foggy and chilly on the day she set out from Catalina; she could scarcely see the boats that would accompany her.

For fifteen hours she swam. She begged to be taken out of the water, but her trainer urged persistence, telling her again and again that she could make it, that the shore was not far away. Physically and emotionally exhausted, Florence finally just stopped swimming and was pulled into the boat, which then headed for the shore—a mere half-mile away.

The next day Florence gave a news conference. What she said, in effect, was this: "I do not want to make excuses for myself. I am the one who asked to be pulled out. But I think that if I could have seen the shore I would have made it." Two months later she proved her point. On a bright and clear day, she plunged back into the sea and swam the distance.[4]

Do we see the shore? Do we have a clear view of where we're heading? Sadly, many of us don't, and as a result, we flounder. We give up. To avoid this pitfall, we need to train ourselves to think eschatologically. That's a mouthful. What does it mean? In very simple terms, it means we must keep two *ages* in view (Ephesians 1:21). The first is the *present age*; it began at creation and continues until Christ's second coming. The second is the *future age*; it began at Christ's first coming and continues into eternity.

Between Christ's first and second comings, therefore, the two ages overlap. At present, we experience the tension of living in two ages—the last days. Another way to describe this tension is to say that we live with the *now* and *not yet* realities of salvation. Christ has inaugurated his kingdom, but he has not yet consummated his kingdom. The implication is that we're saved yet awaiting salvation, adopted yet awaiting adoption, and redeemed yet awaiting redemption. When we understand this *tension*, we're able to weigh our present conditions and circumstances in light of eternal glory.

Several years ago, I lectured for a couple of weeks at a Bible school in the city of Kathmandu, Nepal. From the hotel restaurant, I had a wonderful view of the Himalayas. As I gazed upon them day after day, their enormity had an awe-inspiring effect. They made me feel awfully small. One evening, I sat outside, watching the sun descend behind the snow-capped mountains. As the sky darkened, the stars gradually appeared. From where I sat, the stars were mere specks in the sky—insignificant in comparison to the Himalayas.

But here's a fascinating question: If I had been able to travel to the stars, how would the Himalayas have appeared from that vantage point? Do you see where I'm going with this? We can easily and quickly lose perspective on our journey homeward, and allow our circumstances to become all-encompassing. To prevent this, we must climb up high to get the lay of the land: we must view things eschatologically.

The Psalms of Ascent are valuable in providing us much-needed perspective, thereby helping us to live in the present age and also in hope of the age to come.

## Travel Tip #4: Stay Focused on the Mystery

What mystery? I'm referring to God's providence—a recurring theme throughout the Psalms of Ascent. When we speak of God's providence, we're simply affirming the fact that God "works all things according to the counsel of his will" (Ephesians 1:11). Ultimately, we confess that this truth is a mystery, because it contains far more than our finite minds can grasp. (For a brief discussion of some of the complexities attached to this doctrine, see the Appendix.)

The fact that God's providence exceeds human comprehension shouldn't surprise us. Can we search the deep things of God? We can't search the One who dwells in unapproachable light—the One no human has seen or can see (1 Timothy 6:15–16). We can sooner contain the sun in a small cup or the ocean in a small shell than God in our limited understanding. Our mind can't contain the One the universe can't contain. We're but small children, standing on the beach, trying in vain to hold the ocean in a bucket. Can we find out the limit of the Almighty (Job 11:7–9)? We have a greater chance of holding the stars in the palm of our hand, measuring the mountains on a scale, gathering the oceans in a thimble, and balancing the world's skyscrapers on a needle than we do of finding out the limit of the Almighty.

It's higher than heaven, deeper than sheol, longer than the earth, and broader than the sea. Heaven is high but limited; sheol is deep but restricted; the earth is long but bounded; and the sea is broad but contained. God alone is unlimited, unrestricted, unbounded, and uncontained.

With this incomprehensible God before us, we take great comfort in the realization that he "works all things according to the counsel of his will"—even if his providence is often inscrutable. Moreover, he works all things together for the good of his people (Romans 8:28). We rest in the conviction that this great God rules the universe (his general providence) for the benefit of his church (his special providence). This conviction takes center stage in the Psalms of Ascent. It shapes the perspective of the psalmists at every turn and imparts spiritual fortitude in the midst of all their troubles.

## Summary

That's it—four travel tips for navigating these fifteen psalms. Admittedly, our journey will be a little more complicated than traveling from Toronto to Orlando. As already mentioned, it's fraught with joys and sorrows, pleasant valleys and perilous mountains, encouraging gains and crippling losses. At times, the wind is in our sails and the sun is on our backs; at other times, we feel like a small vessel at the mercy of a great tempest. Whatever our condition, I'm certain these *tips* will keep us moving in the right direction. For that reason, I'll be sure to remind you of them at numerous points along the way.

One final note before we start out: an interesting feature of the Psalms of Ascent is that we don't know the precise context for most of them. In other words, we don't know the exact circumstances that gave rise to most of these psalms. I'm inclined to think the Holy Spirit has fashioned them this way, so that we can immediately identify with the psalmist's experience and apply it to our own context. And so, my approach will be very straightforward, I will seek to give the sense of each psalm while mainly focusing on its significance for our journey home. With all that said, it's time to begin.

# 1

# Pursuing Peace

## *Psalm 120*

[1] In my distress I called to the LORD, and he answered me.
[2] Deliver me, O LORD, from lying lips, from a deceitful tongue.
[3] What shall be given to you, and what more shall be done to you, you deceitful tongue?
[4] A warrior's sharp arrows, with glowing coals of the broom tree!
[5] Woe to me, that I sojourn in Meshech, that I dwell among the tents of Kedar!
[6] Too long have I had my dwelling among those who hate peace.
[7] I am for peace, but when I speak, they are for war!

I realize that might initially sound strange, so let me explain. Many years ago, a colleague secretly began misrepresenting my views, motives, and decisions to others. These seeds of slander soon ripened into false accusations. Sadly, some people accepted these misrepresentations without a moment's hesitation. That was bad enough, but even worse was that I knew what was happening but could do nothing about it. I couldn't control or contain the whispers or falsehoods. There was no forum for setting the record straight and no mechanism for dealing with the underlying issues.

I was trapped—the victim of a smear campaign. As I look back, that was one of my most difficult seasons in my years of pastoral ministry—and in my entire life. I'm certain you can empathize with what I'm describing—most of you know from bitter experience what it's like to be trapped in *the prison cell of words*.

Psalm 120 addresses this painful dilemma. The psalmist begins, "In my distress I called to the LORD, and he answered me" (v. 1). Here, the psalmist provides a brief summary of his experience, emphasizing three simple facts. First, he says he was in "distress," a term that literally refers to a closed or confined space. Thus, the psalmist is saying he felt like a caged or trapped animal. He couldn't flee or fight. The image is one of complete helplessness. Second, he says he "called" to God in his distress. Why? Evidently, he knew his predicament was beyond his power to resolve. Recognizing his inability to do anything about it, he looked to God as his only hope. Third, he says that God "answered" his prayer.

That's how the psalmist summarizes his experience. It's brief. I don't know about you, but it leaves me asking a number of questions. What caused him such distress? What did he actually say as he called out to God? How did God answer him? Thankfully, he fills in the missing details in the remainder of the psalm.

### The Psalmist's Distress (v. 2)

"Deliver me, O LORD, from lying lips, from a deceitful tongue."

The cause of the psalmist's distress is now obvious—people are speaking evil of him. We don't know exactly what they're saying, but we do know the nature of their messages: deceit, libel, slander, rumor, falsehood, defamation, misrepresentation. Do you get the picture? The psalmist is the victim of character assassination, and he's in distress because he's helpless to do anything about it. He can't defend himself, nor can he go on the offensive. He feels like a trapped animal—he can neither flee nor fight. These verbal attacks have become his prison cell.

Has this ever happened to you?

Have you ever been slandered in secret? Have you ever been the victim of a smear campaign? Have people ever spread lies about you and left you unable to stop the bleeding? You were given no opportunity to respond—to set the record straight. Did these verbal attacks become your prison cell?

Have you ever been ridiculed in public? "You're useless." "You're hideous." "You're dense." What did our mothers teach us? "Sticks and stones may break my bones, but names will never hurt me." I recall hearing those words many times on the school playground, and I'm sure many adults still recite this little ditty in one form or another. But with all due respect to our mothers, they were wrong. Words can inflict far greater damage than sticks. They can maim for life and become a prison cell where there's no chance of escape.

Without doubt, the tongue is an invaluable instrument. It comforts, instructs, soothes, inspires, appeases, informs, encourages, and corrects. Without it, a mother can't sing lullabies to her children, a teacher can't instruct her students, a lieutenant can't direct his troops, a lawyer can't defend her clients, and a preacher can't proclaim the gospel. Yet despite its many accomplishments, the tongue is an instrument that can be seriously misused and abused.

James says the tongue is powerful (James 3:3–5). We direct a horse with a small bit and a ship with a small rudder. These small things guide, control, and influence enormous objects—wielding influence out of all proportion to their size. "So also the tongue is a small member," warns James, "yet it boasts of great things."

James also says the tongue is dangerous (James 3:5–6). He declares, "How great a forest is set ablaze by such a small fire!" Often times, the cause of a forest fire is something insignificant. A mere spark quickly gives rise to a blaze, which rages for days, weeks, or months, consuming thousands of acres of vegetation and whatever else stands in its way. Likewise, the tongue is a spark, which sets "on fire the entire course of life." It's "a world of unrighteousness," which quickly descends into malice, deceit, gossip, bitterness, backbiting, and murmuring. It wreaks havoc and creates chaos. It harasses, belittles, and demolishes. It takes no prisoners and spares no one—no matter how innocent. It destroys reputations, friendships, families, ministries, and churches.

Finally, James says the tongue is uncontrollable (James 3:7–8). We're able to tame wild animals such as lions, bears, dolphins, and elephants; but "no human being can tame the tongue." Why? James gives two reasons. First, it's a "restless evil." Animals can be contained in cages, but nothing can contain the tongue. It's impossible to cage it let alone control it. Second, it's "full of deadly poison." Like a snake, the tongue is venomous: its nature is to injure.

Now, let me pause to ask a sobering question: Do we recognize our tendency to fall prey to this sin? Is it possible we're guilty of causing "distress" in others' lives? Is our tongue full of jealousy and bitterness? Is our throat an open grave? Are our words malicious and slanderous? Are they slowly beating others down? Have we left victims lying in the wake of our verbal barrages? Are our words like a seasoned boxer's combination of jabs, hooks, crosses, and uppercuts? If so, we would do well to remember that our speech is the infallible test of true religion: "If anyone thinks he is religious and does not bridle his tongue but deceives his heart, this person's religion is worthless" (James 1:26).

We would also do well to remember that the tongue is the difference between heaven and hell: "I tell you, on the day of judgment people will give account for every careless word they speak, for by your words you will be justified, and by your words you will be condemned" (Matthew 12:37). Why does Christ say this? His point is that words are the best indicator of what's in the heart: "Out of the abundance of the heart the mouth speaks" (Matthew 12:34). In other words, whatever grows abundantly in our heart eventually finds its way into our speech.

We can't curb our tongue because we can't change our heart; but Christ can do both. Through the gospel, he humbles the proud heart and breaks the stubborn heart, enabling meekness, kindness, and gentleness to grow there. Through the gospel, he turns bitterness into sweetness, transforming "corrupting" words into edifying words (Ephesians 4:29).

## The Psalmist's Prayer (v. 2)

"Deliver me, O LORD, from lying lips, from a deceitful tongue."

Interestingly, the psalmist addresses God as the "LORD." This name is significant because it declares the *nature* of God's being. "God said unto Moses, 'I AM WHO I AM.' And he said, 'Say this to the people of Israel, "I AM has sent me to you"'" (Exodus 3:14). God is I AM, meaning his duration knows nothing of past or future because he "inhabits eternity" (Isaiah 57:15).

In addition to indicating his eternality, God's name also points to his immutability. James writes, "Every good gift and every perfect gift is from above, coming down from the Father of lights with whom there is no variation or shadow due to change" (James 1:17). The "lights" (sun, moon, and stars) cast shadows as they move in their orbit. These shadows are constantly changing. But God—"the Father of lights"—isn't like that; because of his nature, he can't change. There are no processes within him or forces outside him that can cause him to change. "I the LORD do not change" (Malachi 3:6).

Edward Pearse sums up the significance of this wonderful truth: "[God] is forever the same, unchangeable in greatness, unchangeable in goodness, unchangeable in wisdom, unchangeable in power, unchangeable in holiness, unchangeable in faithfulness, unchangeable in fullness and sufficiency. He is in every way an unchangeable God. What he was, he is; what he is, he will be forever."[1]

This unchanging God is the Creator of all things. Paul declares, "For from him and through him and to him are all things" (Romans 11:36). All things flow from God and to God, meaning he's the cause *by which* all things exist, the means *through which* all things exist, and the end *for which* all things exist. This unchanging God is also the Governor of all things. Paul declares, "[God] is over all and through all and in all" (Ephesians 4:6). Here's a little grammar lesson: there are three prepositions in this verse. First, God is *over* all. This is his *majestic* presence; he "sits in the heavens" (Psalm 2:4), where he gives the fullest manifestation of his glory. Second, God is *through* all. This is his *providential* presence; he isn't removed from creation but sustains, appoints, and governs everything. He upholds "the universe by the word of his power" (Hebrews 1:3). Third, God is *in* all. This is his *essential* presence; he's present in all places at all times. "Am I a God at hand, declares the LORD, and not a God afar off? Can a man hide himself in secret places so that I cannot see him? declares the LORD. Do I not fill heaven and earth? declares the LORD" (Jeremiah 23:23–24).

This is the God that the psalmist calls upon in his hour of distress; he draws near to this boundless and limitless God—the Creator and Governor of all things. He addresses this incomparable and incomprehensible God in prayer: "Deliver me, O LORD." What an amazing privilege! He who is I AM has designed prayer to be what Jonathan Edwards describes as the "antecedent to the bestowment of mercy."[2] That is to say, this unchanging God, who is merciful to his people, has ordained prayer as the way we request what he has promised to bestow.

### The Lord's Answer (vv. 3–7)

In this chapter, Psalm 120, God answers the psalmist's prayer, but not in the way we probably expect. The psalmist prays for deliverance from "lying lips" and "a deceitful tongue." Naturally, we expect God will respond by removing the psalmist's bitter opponents and restoring the psalmist's good name. Surprisingly (for us anyway), that isn't what happens. There's no storybook ending.

God answers the psalmist's prayer not by changing his circumstances but by changing his perspective. To put it another way, God answers the psalmist's prayer not by delivering him from his problems but by delivering him from *himself.* How? In short, God keeps the psalmist from the snare of bitterness, guards him from the spirit of vengeance, and enables him to seek peace with his enemies while awaiting divine justice. All of this is evident from what the psalmist declares in verses 3–7.

*First, the psalmist anticipates justice.* "What shall be given to you, and what more shall be done to you, you deceitful tongue? A warrior's sharp arrows, with glowing coals of the broom tree!" (vv. 3–4). Apparently, the broom (or juniper) tree was a popular source of firewood in ancient times because it burned longer than other types of wood. And so, the psalmist mentions it to stress the destructive power of these blazing arrows. That much is clear. The difficulty lies in trying to determine what he intends the blazing arrows to represent.

It's possible the psalmist is using this vivid imagery to describe the destruction inflicted *by* the "deceitful tongue." Agreeing with this view, John Calvin states, "The tongues of these slanderers were inflamed with the burning heat of fire, and, as it were, dipped in deadly poison."[3] But it's also possible the psalmist is using this vivid imagery to describe the destruction inflicted *on* the "deceitful tongue." In other words, he could be saying that God's judgment upon the psalmist's enemies will be like "a warrior's sharp arrows, with glowing coals of the broom tree."

Either way, the psalmist's main point remains the same: he anticipates justice. "What shall be given to you, and what more shall be done to you, you deceitful tongue?" The psalmist's circumstances might not change; in fact, his predicament might even grow worse; but he rests in the fact that eventually God will right all wrongs.

*Second, the psalmist pursues peace.* "Woe to me, that I sojourn in Meshech, that I dwell among the tents of Kedar! Too long have I had my dwelling among those who hate peace. I am for peace, but when I speak, they are for war!" (vv. 5–7). The psalmist laments that he dwells in Meshech (Asia Minor) and Kedar (Arabia). How can he dwell simultaneously in two places which are hundreds of miles apart? He can't. He's speaking metaphorically of his enemies, who are actually fellow Israelites. His point is that living among those who hate peace is like living in the godless places of Meshech and Kedar. Yet, despite the opposition and frustration, he doesn't return slander with slander, malice with malice, deceit with deceit, rumor with rumor, or lie with lie. Rather, he remains committed to the pursuit of peace. He doesn't merely refrain from evil but seeks to win over his enemies while waiting patiently upon God.

That's how the psalmist's prayer for deliverance is answered by God. Again, God doesn't deliver the writer from his problems, but from *himself*. God delivers the psalmist by changing his perspective, thereby preserving him from sin.

We, too, need that kind of deliverance when we're on the receiving end of verbal attacks. Let's be honest: we usually respond sinfully when sinned against. Don't we? When it's all said and done, we're not too different from Shylock in Shakespeare's *Merchant of Venice*. If you're unfamiliar with this classic, let me fill you in. Antonio (a Venetian merchant) has belittled Shylock on several occasions, and Shylock is keeping a mental record of every slight as he secretly plots his revenge. One day, Antonio comes to Shylock to request a loan for a commercial enterprise. Shylock grants it—interest free but with one condition: if Antonio fails to pay the loan, he must forfeit a pound of his flesh. As the story unfolds, Antonio's ships are lost at sea, his commercial enterprise falls apart, and he's unable to pay his debt. Shylock rejects all pleas for clemency. He won't hear of granting Antonio additional time to gather the money. He won't even accept a friend's offer to pay twice what Antonio owes. Why? He wants Antonio's pound of flesh!

Are we like that? When someone wrongs us, our first impulse is to keep a mental record—tucked away for just the right moment. We feel entitled to a little payback. Do any of the following scenarios sound familiar? My spouse said something insensitive, so I'm going to employ the silent treatment; after all, I need to send her a clear message. My boss spoke harshly when he corrected me. Well, I'm going to make sure everyone in the office knows what a loser he is; he needs to learn a little humility anyway. My son contradicted me in front of guests. I'm going to make sure I punish him so that he never embarrasses me like that again. My sibling criticized me when I was fifteen years old. I'm going to bring it up over Thanksgiving dinner (ten years later) to embarrass her in front of everyone. I'll do it in a light-hearted manner, of course.

Paul exhorts, "Repay no one evil for evil. . . . If possible, so far as it depends on you, live peaceably with all. Beloved, never avenge yourselves, but leave it to the wrath of God, for it is written, 'Vengeance is mine, I will repay, says the Lord'" (Romans 12:17–19). This passage offers an excellent summary of the psalmist's attitude in the midst of his distress. He prays for deliverance from those who've wronged him, refuses to avenge himself, seeks to live in peace, and leaves his predicament to God.

## Conclusion

When we step back for a moment, we discover that this psalm ultimately points us to Christ. *See Travel Tip #2.* As we read the Gospels, we see Christ in great distress on account of what people say about him. They misinterpret and misrepresent him, mock him, and malign him. They accuse him of breaking the Sabbath, rejecting the Scriptures, dishonoring the temple, serving the Devil, and supporting the Romans. They even accuse him of blasphemy. As he suffers in agony, they scoff: "If you are the Son of God, come down from the cross" (Matthew 27:39–40).

How does Christ respond to it all? "When he was reviled, he did not revile in return; when he suffered, he did not threaten, but continued entrusting himself to him who judges justly. He himself bore our sins in his body on the tree, that we might die to sin and live to righteousness" (1 Peter 2:23–24). Here we have it: rather than avenging himself, Christ chose to entrust himself "to him who judges justly." He did so because he had a glorious end in view: the cross. And this must be our focus when we find ourselves in the psalmist's predicament. *See Travel Tip #1.*

The cross enables us to escape a prison cell of words. How? It shapes our identity. As Christians, we're one with Christ in his death, burial, and resurrection. Because we're one with him, we're justified in God's sight and adopted into God's family. That makes us God's *beloved.* For this reason, we don't define ourselves on the basis of what others say about us, but on the basis of what God says about us. And that frees us from the prison cell of words.

The cross also enables us to offer forgiveness to those who hate peace. When we contemplate the cross, we're crushed to the ground and overwhelmed by God's love for us. Moreover, we're compelled to quench our desire for personal vengeance and extend compassion to others. By God's grace, we seek peace with all people so far as it depends on us.

Finally, the cross enables us to persevere in the land of Meshech and Kedar. We're surrounded by those who hate peace. But Christ is enthroned in glory (Revelation 1:12–18). His hair is like white snow, and his feet are like burnished bronze. His voice is like the roar of many waters, and his face is like the sun shining in full strength. He walks in the midst of his people, calling to us: "Fear not, I am the first and the last, and the living one. I died, and behold I am alive forevermore" (vv. 17–18). We're certain that deliverance will come—fully and finally. Whatever verbal attacks we suffer now, we know Christ will right all wrongs. He alone will have the final word.

## Questions

1. What lies behind all speech?

2. Why will our words either justify or condemn us?

3. What does James say about the tongue?

4. Have you hurt someone with your words? If so, do you need to ask his/her forgiveness?

5. When you speak inappropriately, what are some of the underlying causes?

6. What should your speech look like? See Eph. 4:15, 25, 29, 32; 5:4; Col. 3:8–9, 15–17.

7. What is the only remedy for curbing/controlling the tongue?

8. Has someone hurt you with his/her words? If so, how should you respond?

9. In what ways can you empathize with the psalmist?

10. How does Christ deliver His people from the prison cell of words? Present? Future?

11. How can you turn this psalm into a prayer? List specific requests.

# 2

# Seeking Help

## *Psalm 121*

¹ I lift up my eyes to the hills. From where does my help come?
² My help comes from the LORD, who made heaven and earth.
³ He will not let your foot be moved; he who keeps you will not slumber.
⁴ Behold, he who keeps Israel will neither slumber nor sleep.
⁵ The LORD is your keeper; the LORD is your shade on your right hand.
⁶ The sun shall not strike you by day, nor the moon by night.
⁷ The LORD will keep you from all evil; he will keep your life.
⁸ The LORD will keep your going out and your coming in from this time forth and forevermore.


In *The Pilgrim's Progress*, John Bunyan traces Christian's sojourn from the City of Destruction to the Celestial City, chronicling his many experiences along the way. At one point, Christian and fellow pilgrim Hopeful notice a pleasant meadow that appears to run parallel to the narrow path they're traveling. Thinking it will ease their difficult journey, they decide to climb over the wall to walk in the meadow.

Initially, all's well, but soon the storm gathers, the sky darkens, and the rain descends. By morning, they're completely lost. To make matters worse, they stumble upon Giant Despair, who captures them, beats them, and imprisons them in Doubting Castle, where all hope is lost. After languishing for days, Christian and Hopeful decide to spend the night in prayer. As day breaks, Christian cries, "What a fool am I, thus to lie in a stinking dungeon, when I may as well walk at liberty? I have a key in my bosom, called *Promise*, that I am persuaded will open any lock in *Doubting Castle*."[1] Within moments, Christian and Hopeful are unlocking chains and doors. Free of Giant Despair and Doubting Castle, they scramble back to the narrow way.

All of us struggle with doubt. At times, the struggle begins because of our own carelessness. That was the case with Christian and Hopeful. The path was difficult, and the meadow seemed pleasant. Following the desires of the flesh, they climbed over the wall. We face the same temptation. The Christian journey is difficult, and we can easily compromise in a misguided attempt to make things easier. When we do, doubt is never far behind.

Suffering can also lead to doubt. It comes in many forms: illness, slander, estrangement, opposition, poverty, sorrow, unemployment, pain, abandonment, danger—to name but a few. We desperately want to be free of these things, yet they often persist. There's no prospect of change and no hope of resolution. Day after day, we feel like a drowning man, simply trying to keep our head above water. A feeling of helplessness takes hold, and doubt follows.

The only key that unlocks the prison cell of such doubt and despair is God's promise: "I will never leave you nor forsake you" (Hebrews 13:5). God's promise of protection nourishes our hope, enabling us to persevere in the midst of dire circumstances. And that brings us to Psalm 121.

## The Psalmist's Question (v. 1)

"I lift up my eyes to the hills. From where does my help come?"

What does the psalmist mean when he says he lifts up his eyes to the hills? What hills? Grammatically, there are two possibilities. First, it's possible he's identifying the hills as *the place where he finds help*. How so? The city of Jerusalem is located in the hill country, and the temple (God's house) stands in Jerusalem. Therefore, when the psalmist says he lifts his eyes to the hills, he might be expressing his confidence that God will help him.

Second, it's possible he's identifying the hills as *the reason he needs help*. That might seem strange to us since we don't normally travel by foot, but the hills are a harsh reality for the psalmist. They're menacing and threatening. They're known for unpredictable weather patterns. They're the hiding place for rebels and robbers and the hunting ground for predators and scavengers. Their terrain is challenging and unforgiving—fraught with rock falls and other hazards.

Either way, the psalmist knows he needs help. He doesn't provide any specifics, but simply asks, "From where does my help come?" Perhaps you've asked that question on occasion. Perhaps you're asking that question right now.

### The Psalmist's Answer (v. 2)

"My help comes from the LORD, who made heaven and earth."

Of all the things he could say about God, why does the psalmist choose to emphasize his work of creation? Why is this so important to him? The answer is simple: God's work of creation declares his infinite power. We can't create *out of nothing* a tree, bush, flower, or even a blade of grass. We can't produce *out of nothing* a rock, shell, pebble, or even a grain of sand. We can alter matter—its form, size, shape, appearance, etc. But we can't make matter when there is none. God can. "The universe was created by the word of God, so that what is seen was not made out of things that are visible" (Heb. 11:3). This verse expresses two important facts concerning the origin of the universe: God created it by his word; and God created it out of nothing.

Amazingly, God continues to uphold what he created. *See Travel Tip #4.* The power that produced all things out of nothing preserves all things from returning to nothing. If he were to suspend his influence, the fire wouldn't burn, the eye wouldn't see, the sun wouldn't shine, the wind wouldn't blow, the hand wouldn't move, the bird wouldn't fly, the grass wouldn't grow. It's impossible for any part of creation to exist for a moment apart from him. He holds all things together. According to J. B. Lightfoot, God "is the principle of cohesion in the universe. He impresses upon creation that unity and solidarity which makes it a *cosmos* instead of a *chaos*."[2] He holds the planets in their orbit, sends the rain to replenish the earth, sustains the beasts of the field and the birds of the air, upholds the clouds as they pass across the sky, and brings forth every bud, every leaf, every fruit, every blossom, and every flower. He gives being to all things: "In him we live and move and have our being" (Acts 17:28).

This God "looks on the earth and it trembles, [he] touches the mountains and they smoke" (Psalm 104:32). A mere glance produces earthquakes, and a mere touch produces volcanoes. If these slight impulses from God cause such devastation, what is the full effect of his power? By his power, God does whatever he pleases. He isn't only powerful but "great in power" (Job 37:23). He isn't only strong but "mighty in strength" (Job 9:4).

This God "determines the number of the stars; he gives to all of them their names" (Psalm 147:4). Apparently, in the time it takes me to snap my fingers, light circles the earth seven times. Traveling at that speed, if the sun were the size of a pea, it would take ten billion years to reach the edge of the universe. How long would it take traveling at a realistic speed? How long would it take given the sun's actual size? We can't get our mind around the computation. Some astronomers estimate that there are more stars in the universe than grains of sand on the earth's beaches. Here are two wonders: God can compute that number, and God can invent that number of names.

This is where the psalmist looks for help. He turns to the only One who *can* help. He turns to the One whose power is boundless. And that's where we must turn in times of trouble, strengthening our confidence in God by reminding ourselves of this unassailable truth: "that he *made heaven and earth*, and he who did that can do anything."[3]

## The Psalmist's Sermon (vv. 3–8)

Until this point, the psalmist has used the first person singular, but, beginning in verse 3, he changes to the second person singular. Why? It's possible he wrote this psalm for Israel to sing responsively—

perhaps the people would sing verses 1–2 and a priest (or someone else) would sing verses 3–8.

But it's also possible that the shift in person indicates that the psalmist is now speaking to himself. Why would he do that? Simply put, he's struggling to relate two truths in his mind. The first is that *his* help comes from God who made heaven and earth. The second is that the God who made heaven and earth is *his* keeper. In other words, he's struggling to take to heart the idea that the power who made the universe is the power who keeps him. In verses 3–8, he seeks to press this point upon himself, approaching it from three angles.

## The Maker of Heaven and Earth Keeps His People in All Places (vv. 3–4)

"He will not let your foot be moved; he who keeps you will not slumber. Behold, he who keeps Israel will neither slumber nor sleep."

When Elijah faces the false prophets on Mt. Carmel, he challenges them to call upon Baal to send fire to consume their sacrifice. They call and call in vain. Elijah begins to ridicule them: "Cry aloud, for he is a god; either he is musing, or he is relieving himself, or he is on a journey, or perhaps he is asleep and must be awakened" (1 Kings 18:27). What's Elijah doing here? He's ascribing human actions to Baal, in order to demonstrate the utter absurdity of those who worship a finite god.

We encounter the same absurdity in the gods of Greek mythology: Zeus, Poseidon, Athena, Apollo, and the rest. When we read the accounts of these gods, we soon discover that they're vain, petty, selfish, moody, and unpredictable. All of these traits are apparent as they compete with one another to influence the course of human history. It doesn't take long to discover that these so-called gods are simply human beings with supernatural powers.

The psalmist's point is that God isn't a glorified human being. On the contrary, he's the Maker of heaven and earth, meaning he's infinite in power. The implication is obvious: "He will not let your foot be moved." When the terrain is treacherous, the slightest slip can be perilous; but God watches over the psalmist. He keeps his people in all places.

## The Maker of Heaven and Earth Keeps His People in All Conditions (vv. 5–6)

"The LORD is your keeper; the LORD is your shade on your right hand. The sun shall not strike you by day, nor the moon by night."

By "shade," the psalmist literally means *shadow*. He might be thinking of the shadow cast by a tree or some other object, providing relief on a hot summer's day; or he might be thinking of his own shadow. Recently, my youngest daughter discovered her shadow. She was mesmerized as it responded to her every action and followed her every movement. She couldn't escape it—no matter how hard she tried. That seems to be the psalmist's point. He's affirming that God is like his shadow—always present.

Since he's always present, God protects his people: "The sun shall not strike you by day nor the moon by night." If we aren't careful in the hot summer sun, we can suffer sunstroke. At one time, people believed there was such a thing as being "moonstruck"—suffering the negative influence of lunar rays. (That's the origin of our term *lunatic*, by the way.) But the psalmist's point isn't that God keeps him from the ill effects of the sun and moon, but that God keeps him from the dangers of night and day. He keeps his people in all conditions.

## The Maker of Heaven and Earth Keeps His People in All Seasons (vv. 7–8)

"The LORD will keep you from all evil; he will keep your life. The LORD will keep your going out and your coming in from this time forth and forevermore."

The expressions "going out" and "coming in" are synonyms for life and death. The psalmist is saying that God keeps him throughout the course of his life. What does God keep him from? "All evil." Now, how are we to understand that? Does God really keep his people from all evil? Did God keep Joseph from all evil? He spent years in jail. Did God keep Naomi from all evil? She buried a husband and two sons. Did God keep Jonathan from all evil? He died on a lonely hill at the edge of a Philistine sword. Did God keep David from all evil? He spent years fleeing from Saul. Did God keep Paul from all evil? He suffered shipwrecks, imprisonments, and beatings. In what sense does God keep the psalmist from all evil?

To answer this, we must begin by acknowledging that there's something far worse than losing our job, health, money, reputation, or even our life. These things are types of temporal evil. What's worse than these things? Ultimate evil: the loss of God. What's the loss of temporal things when compared to losing God—the One at whose "right hand are pleasures forevermore" (Psalm 16:11)? What's the loss of these things when compared to an eternity in the furnace of hell—an agony that never ends, a pain that never ceases, a sorrow that never subsides, a horror that never lessens, and a torment that never departs?

The greatness of any loss is measured by the value of what's lost. If God is incomparable, then the loss of him must be incomparable. If he's infinite, then the loss of him must be infinite. If he's incomprehensible, then the loss of him must be incomprehensible.

The psalmist's point is that God keeps him from ultimate evil: the loss of God. God is the Maker of heaven and earth; his power is infinite. Therefore, he keeps the psalmist's "going out and coming in from this time forth and forevermore." He keeps his people in all seasons.

## Conclusion

God keeps us in all places, all conditions, and all seasons. As Peter writes, "By God's power [we] are being guarded through faith for a salvation ready to be revealed in the last time" (1 Peter 1:5). Here, Peter mentions three important truths which parallel the psalmist's hope. First, God is guarding us by his power—he's our keeper. Second, God is guarding us "for a salvation to be revealed in the last time." He protects us from ultimate evil, ensuring our final salvation. Third, God is guarding us "through faith." His infinite power keeps us unto salvation by sustaining our faith.

Repeatedly, the psalmist states that God is his *keeper* (vv. 3, 4, 5, 7, 8). His repetition seems superfluous until we remember how difficult it can be to trust God when the hills are menacing and threatening. Just like the psalmist, we struggle to live in the reality of what we know to be true.

At times, our struggle is related to our thoughts. We have deep-rooted ideas of how we think God should work. But his ways rarely match our ways, so then what happens? We implode emotionally. We think something is wrong with God, or something is wrong with us. We begin to doubt and despair. In these times, we need to remember that deliverance from suffering only comes fully and finally in glory. *See Travel Tip #3.* To put it another way, we need to remember that the Christian life always *ends* well but it doesn't always *go* well. In times of difficulty, we lift up our eyes to our God, reminding ourselves that he's in control. Despite changing circumstances, his love for his people doesn't change, and this love is the most valuable thing in life.

At times, our struggle is related to our feelings. When difficulties arise, our emotions often take over, exacerbating the problem. Years ago, I was flying in the front seat of a small plane over the country of Angola. As we passed through dense cloud and lost all visibility, I turned to the pilot, and somewhat sheepishly asked, "What now?" His response: "What do you mean, 'What now'? I keep doing what I always do. I trust this plane's guidance systems." The temptation for any pilot in the midst of thick cloud is to fall back on his senses. If he does, it will always get him into trouble.

When we are in the cloud, when we are facing difficult times in life, far too many of us decide to navigate by our feelings. The result is always disastrous. We must trust God's guidance system: his precepts and promises. Faith is fixed on objective historical facts and objective biblical promises—not subjective emotional feelings.

At times, the hills are daunting, and the darkness closes all around. Our knees buckle under the pressure, and our shoulders droop under the weight. We succumb to doubt. But here's the key that always unlocks the chains of doubt and despair: "My help comes from the LORD, who made heaven and earth."

## Questions

1. What is the underlying cause of doubt and despair?

2. How can our *thoughts* and *feelings* deepen our despair?

3. Where does the psalmist look? Why?

4. How does the psalmist preach to himself?

5. In what sense is God our keeper?

6. How does this psalm apply to your present circumstances?

7. Has God promised us freedom from difficulty? What has He promised us? Give Scripture references.

8. How can you turn this psalm into a prayer? List specific requests.

# 3

# Prizing Community

## *Psalm 122*

[1] I was glad when they said to me, "Let us go to the house of the LORD!"
[2] Our feet have been standing within your gates, O Jerusalem!
[3] Jerusalem—built as a city that is bound firmly together,
[4] to which the tribes go up, the tribes of the LORD, as was decreed for Israel, to give thanks to the name of the LORD.
[5] There thrones for judgment were set, the thrones of the house of David.
[6] Pray for the peace of Jerusalem! "May they be secure who love you!
[7] Peace be within your walls and security within your towers!"
[8] For my brothers and companions' sake I will say, "Peace be within you!"
[9] For the sake of the house of the LORD our God, I will seek your good.

Kevin DeYoung has formulated an interesting, if somewhat grisly, term to describe a current trend within the church: *decorpulation*.[1] We're all familiar with the meaning of *decapitation*—the removal of the head from the body. Well, *decorpulation* emphasizes the other side of the equation—the removal of the body from the head.

DeYoung uses this term to describe those professing Christians who claim to belong to the head—Christ—while rejecting, or at least sorely neglecting, the body—the church. These people claim to be followers of Christ, yet they see no need to pursue, cultivate, or maintain any connection or involvement in a local church. We can only describe their level of commitment as casual. I'm guessing you know people who fall into this category.

What has led to this growing trend? Good question. I have a theory you might disagree with, but please hear me out. Personally, I believe a significant part of the problem lies in our society's increasing superficiality, which has spilled over into the ranks of the church. This lack of depth is the result of numerous factors—far too many to cover here, but I can at least give you a sampling.[2]

For starters, our society loves technology. It began with television, blossomed with the computer, mushroomed with the Internet, and exploded with wireless. Don't misunderstand me—I'm not saying there's anything wrong with any of those things per se. For the most part, technology is morally neutral; it can be good or bad depending on how it is used. The problem is that nowadays most people are connected 24/7. As a result, they're slowly disengaging from the real world and using technology in such a way that they're physically present while mentally absent. I attended a church luncheon recently and observed an older couple sitting at a table with four or five youths who each had his or her nose glued to some sort of electronic device. Their meal together was void of any meaningful discussion or communication. (I think I heard one of them ask someone to pass the salt, but that doesn't count as meaningful.) I wish this were a rarity, but it isn't. And I can't help but wonder what the long-term consequences will be for this kind of relational—and generational—detachment.

Our society also loves novelty. Most people accept the notion that we're advancing without ever questioning it. The mind-boggling rate of technological innovation in recent years has contributed in large part to this perception, because people tend to equate technology with progress. This has served to reinforce our society's conviction that we were bound to tradition and superstition in the past, in some vaguely defined era known as the Dark Ages, but now we've seen the light. For this reason, most people don't view themselves as stewards of the past. Why would they when they don't think the past offers anything worth protecting or preserving? Their interest is limited to the next *upgrade*. This trend has resulted in a measure of historical disconnectedness.

Our society also loves equality. "We're all equal." That's a catchy phrase and certainly the mantra of many. But what do we mean by it? If we mean we're all equal in worth or value in God's sight, then it's true; however, if we mean we're all equal in gifts, skills, and abilities, then it's wrong. Yet the latter is the prevailing mindset, and it has contributed to a growing culture of entitlement. Some people think they're entitled to what others possess. Some think they're entitled to a certain salary, position, or way of living. Still others think they're entitled to pontificate on whatever subject they like—after all, their opinion is just as valid and valuable as anyone else's, regardless of their academic aptitude or intellectual capacity. Anthony Selvaggio sums up this ever-increasing sense of entitlement as follows: "We are raising a generation of children who have been deceived by the lie that we all deserve a trophy."[3]

Finally, our society loves prosperity. Many people today approach spending as if it were morally virtuous. We talk about the consumer index, which measures consumer confidence. This infatuation with purchasing and accumulating bespeaks a severely twisted value system. As Carl Trueman rightly explains, "Consumerism is predicated on the idea that life can be fulfilling through acquiring something in the future that one does not have in the present."[4] This means that our consumer-driven society is built on the notion that the key to happiness is found in acquiring the next product—whatever that might be. The world of advertising exists to convince us of this very thing: "What we have now is not enough for happiness."[5] The question of *need* never even enters the equation. The entire system is predicated on greed—and a skewed notion of contentment.

Combined with other contributing factors, these cultural forces have produced a pervading superficiality. Now, we dare not miss this: as God's people, we have not remained untouched by these cultural influences. We're extremely naïve if we think otherwise. Our love affair with technology, novelty, equality, and prosperity now shapes much of modern-day evangelicalism. We stress representation rather than reality, images rather than words, emotion rather than reflection. We're enamored with technique, whereby the message and music have become part of a presentation, package, and product.[6] The chief goal of this product is to attract the largest audience. As a result, the audience (dare I say consumer) has become sovereign.

I believe this dramatic shift in our thinking is part of what accounts for the current trend of *decorpulation*. Far too many of us view the church as a *product*. Our commitment to any product only extends as far as its perceived usefulness to us. Thus, we approach the church with a skewed mental framework, assuming it exists for us—to meet our needs and satisfy our demands. When it fails to deliver, we simply move on. If we're ever going to reverse this trend, we need to re-evaluate our approach to the cultural forces mentioned above. (That topic is well beyond the scope of this chapter.) Of equal importance, we need to rediscover the centrality of the church in God's eternal plan.

And that brings us to Psalm 122. Here, David *goes crazy* over the city of Jerusalem—quite literally. The psalm actually reads like a love letter—an intimate exchange between husband and wife, as David expresses his heartfelt love, esteem, and desire for Jerusalem.

### David's Love for Jerusalem (v. 1)

"I was glad when they said to me, 'Let us go to the house of the LORD!'"

When David penned these words, the temple didn't exist. It wasn't built until the days of his son, Solomon. So what does he mean when he speaks of "the house of the LORD?" He's referring to the tent he erected in Jerusalem to house the Ark of the Covenant (1 Chronicles 16:1). This tent was God's dwelling place among his people.

David expresses his joy as he looks forward to visiting this place. It's the object of his desire—he anticipates being there. It's also the object of his delight—he enjoys being there. He dreams about it, sings about it, and (obviously) writes poetry about it. For David, Jerusalem is the place God puts his name—the place he makes his habitation (Deuteronomy 12:5). Naturally, he longs to be where God is glorified and magnified.

## David's Esteem for Jerusalem (vv. 2–5)

"Our feet have been standing within your gates, O Jerusalem!"

We can picture David standing in the city's center, gazing upon its walls, towers, and ramparts. As he soaks it all in, he's amazed. Why? What grabs his attention? First, Jerusalem is the nation's *religious* center: "Jerusalem—built as a city that is bound firmly together, to which the tribes go up, the tribes of the LORD, as was decreed for Israel, to give thanks to the name of the LORD" (vv. 3–4). David's point is that God appointed Jerusalem as the place where the priests would minister, and the people would gather for worship. Second, Jerusalem is the nation's *political* center: "There thrones for judgment were set, the thrones of the house of David" (v. 5). Here, David celebrates the fact that God appointed Jerusalem as the place where the kings would reign and the people would gather for judgment.

These two offices—priest and king—are united in Jerusalem. That's the principal cause of David's enthusiasm. He doesn't merely esteem the city for its rich history, beautiful architecture, splendid gardens, or cultural refinement, but for the place it holds in the plan of God. To put it in very simple terms, David esteems Jerusalem because God esteems Jerusalem.

## David's Desire for Jerusalem (vv. 6–9)

"Pray for the peace of Jerusalem! May they be secure who love you! Peace be within your walls and security within your towers! For my brothers and companions' sake I will say, 'Peace be within you!' For the sake of the house of the LORD our God, I will seek your good."

David prays for Jerusalem's peace and security. Doubtless, this includes political stability and economic prosperity. Primarily, however, David wants the inhabitants of Jerusalem to enjoy the full blessing of God's presence among them—*shalom*. He expends his time, effort, strength, resources, and abilities in this pursuit. Why? He furnishes two reasons: first, he seeks Jerusalem's good for the sake of his "brothers and companions"; second, he seeks Jerusalem's good for the sake of "the house of the LORD." In other words, his motivation lies in his love for God's people and God's glory. These two factors inspire David's fervent prayer and diligent service.

## Conclusion

Admittedly, we could spend considerable more time studying some of the details in this psalm, but I think we've got the sense of it. The question now is this: What does it have to do with us? After all, David's zeal for "the house of the LORD" (as so powerfully evident in this psalm) seems totally removed from our experience.

In bridging the gap between David and us, we need to recognize that Christ's first advent marked a dramatic shift in God's plan of redemption, as it moved from the age of preparation to the age of fulfillment. *See Travel Tip #2.* As stated in the introduction to this book, the theme of the Old Testament is Christ and his kingdom. At the outset of his public ministry, Christ declared, "The time is fulfilled, and the kingdom of God is at hand" (Mark 1:14). In the days of the patriarchs, this kingdom was promised; in the days of the judges, it was prefigured; in the days of the kings, it was previewed; and in the days of the prophets, it was prophesied. The Old Testament in its entirety—as God's progressive revelation—points to and prepares for Christ and his kingdom.

The implication is that all of the events, rituals, traditions, and ceremonies of the Old Testament constitute a *shadow*, which prepared for the *substance*: Christ (Colossians 2:17). A man's shadow might tell us something about his size and height and give some indication of the length of his hair and nose. It might even reveal what he's wearing—shorts or trousers, shoes or boots, etc. But that's it. If we want to know what this man really looks like, we must look him in the face.

Similarly, the Old Testament is but Christ's shadow. This shadow includes, among other things, the earthly tent, tabernacle, and temple—what David calls "the house of the LORD." Christ, on the other hand, is the substance—"the true tent" (Hebrews 8:2). He isn't *true* as opposed to something that is *false*, but *true* as opposed to that which is *typical*. As God dwelt in the earthly tent (Exodus 29:45), he now dwells in the true tent (Colossians 2:9). As God manifested his glory in the earthly tent (Exodus 40:34), he now manifests his glory in the true tent (John 1:14).

When Christ ascended the mountain, he was "transfigured" before Peter, James, and John (Mark 9:2). The Greek term translated here as *transfigured* is the origin of our English word *metamorphosis*—a change in form. We use it when referring to insects or amphibians, which begin life as a larva and then transform into something else. The most obvious example is the caterpillar, which undergoes metamorphosis, thereby transforming into a butterfly.

On the mountain, Christ undergoes a transformation. He isn't changed in the substance or features of his body. He's changed in that his divine glory becomes visible. God dwells in unapproachable light—the resplendent glory of his holiness (1 Timothy 6:16). This light shines through the veil of Christ's humanity at the moment of his transfiguration. That's why, years later, Peter proclaimed, "We were eyewitnesses of his majesty" (2 Peter 1:16).

In addition to the light, a bright cloud engulfs the mountain. It's the *Shekinah* (dwelling) glory. At the time of the Exodus, God descended in a cloud to guide the Israelites to Canaan. The cloud was a visible manifestation of his dwelling among them. Later, he descended in a cloud to fill the Holy of Holies in the tabernacle and temple, which was then an earthly tent. Again, the cloud was a visible manifestation of God's dwelling among them. Now, the cloud engulfs Christ because "in him the whole fullness of deity dwells bodily" (Colossians 2:9). Christ is the substance—the true tent—and, therefore, the fulfillment of God's promise to dwell among his people.

Now, here's an equally wonderful truth: When the Holy Spirit unites us to Christ, we become "a holy temple in the Lord . . . a dwelling place for God by the Spirit" (Ephesians 2:21–22). That is, God makes us his habitation by virtue of our union with Christ. This has always been his plan. There's an *eternal* union, whereby God the Father set his love upon his people before the foundation of the world. There's also a *historical* union, whereby God the Son became one with God's people in their humanity, fulfilling the duty of the law through his substitutionary life and satisfying the penalty of the law through his substitutionary death. And there's a *mystical* union, whereby God the Spirit unites God's people to Christ. By virtue of this union, everything Christ purchased for them is credited to them.

Because we're united to Christ, we're united to each other, meaning we constitute the church—the body and bride of Christ. Do you see where I'm heading with this? Now, look at Psalm 122 through the lens of Christ and his church. Like David, we gaze in wonder at "the house of the LORD" (vv. 1–2). We behold the priestly and kingly offices bound together in Christ (vv. 3–5). "All our salvation," says John Calvin, "depends upon these two points; first, that Christ has been given to us to be our priest; and, secondly, that he has been established king to govern us."[7] Like David, our prayer for the church is that she might abound in "peace"—the knowledge of God with us, for us, and in us (vv. 6–7). Like David, we're zealous for "the house of the LORD," stirred on by our love for God's people and delight in God's glory (vv. 8–9).

This church stands at the focal point of God's eternal plan. The Father set his love upon her and predestined her for glory. The Son became a man for her; he endured affliction and rejection for her; he wept, bled, pled, and died for her; he purchased her with his own blood. As the hymn writer Samuel Stone so eloquently expresses it:

> The church's one foundation is Jesus Christ her Lord;
> She is His new creation, by Spirit and the Word:
> From heav'n He came and sought her to be His holy bride,
> With His own blood He bought her, and for her life He died.[8]

When we see the church in this light, we soon realize it's impossible to separate the head from the body: *decorpulation*. To be united to Christ is to be united to the church. To be in fellowship with Christ is to be in fellowship with the church. To be committed to Christ is to be committed to the church. To esteem Christ is to esteem the church. To love Christ is to love the church. The church isn't a *product*. It doesn't exist to cater to our whims. It exists for the glory of the triune God.

I don't pretend for one moment that the church is perfect—I realize she's plagued with a plethora of problems. If you've spent any time in a local church, you know it firsthand. This reality can be deflating and discouraging. When Dorothy and her friends finally make it to the Emerald City in *The Wizard of Oz*, the wizard appears as a giant head made of fire and smoke. His voice thunders in their ears. But Toto (Dorothy's dog) pulls back a curtain to reveal an insignificant-looking old man, speaking into a microphone. He's pulling levers and pressing buttons, which produce the awe-inspiring "image" of the wizard. He sees Dorothy and the others staring at him, and quickly speaks into the microphone: "Pay no attention to the man behind the curtain!" But it's too late. The spell is broken. That's often what happens in the church. We have certain expectations about the way things ought to be in church. Suddenly, the curtain is removed, and we see what's really there. The temptation is to become cynical. But we must remember that this imperfect gathering of justified sinners is a local expression of the body of Christ, "the arena for Christian love."[9]

Do we realize what we're doing when we neglect the church? I fear many of us do not. It boils down to this: how we treat the church is how we treat Christ. Dare I say it? I dare. What we think of the church is really what we think of Christ. The two are inseparable: head and body. Christ loves his bride. He married her, thereby becoming one flesh with her. Now, he cherishes and cleanses her; he bestows marvelous gifts and blessings upon her; he guides and protects her; and he longs for the day when he will present her in splendor—spotless before him.

As we journey homeward, we must grasp the church's place in God's eternal plan, and we must seek to love her, esteem her, and desire her.

## Questions

1. Why does David take such delight in Jerusalem?

2. Why did God institute the church?

3. Is the church perfect? Why shouldn't this surprise us?

4.  Do you esteem the church? How?

5.  Are you a member of a local church? What does your membership look like?

6.  In what ways are you currently serving others?

7.  Are you accountable to anyone in your church?

8.  If you left your church today, would anyone notice?

9.  Do you practice hospitality? How?

10. How can you turn this psalm into a prayer? List specific requests.

# 4

# Handling Opposition

## *Psalm 123*

[1] To you I lift up my eyes, O you who are enthroned in the heavens!
[2] Behold, as the eyes of servants look to the hand of their master,
as the eyes of a maidservant to the hand of her mistress,
so our eyes look to the LORD our God, till he has mercy upon us.
[3] Have mercy upon us, O LORD, have mercy upon us,
for we have had more than enough of contempt.
[4] Our soul has had more than enough of the scorn of those who are
at ease, of the contempt of the proud.

Christ declares, "The world cannot hate you, but it hates me because I testify about it that its works are evil" (John 7:7). What's the
world? It's a certain way of *thinking* and *behaving*. "Worldliness,"
explains David Wells, "is that system of values and beliefs, behavior
and expectations, in any given culture that have at their center the
fallen human being, and that relegate to their periphery any thought
about God."[1]

That definition is clear enough. Christ's point is that this "system
of value and beliefs" is antithetical to him. This animosity has a long
history, extending all the way back to the fall, when God promised
to put enmity between the seed of the serpent and the seed of the
woman (Genesis 3:15). The seed of the serpent is fallen humanity
(that is, the world), whereas the seed of the woman is Christ and

all who are united to him. Ever since the fall, there has been enmity between these two seeds because—simply put—they're diametrically opposed to one another.

Has anyone ever experienced enmity like Christ? On one occasion, he declared, "They hated me without a cause" (John 15:25). Here's a remarkable (and often overlooked) truth: he continues to experience opposition through his spiritual body—the church. Because of our identification with Christ, we often become the object of the world's hatred. Richard Baxter affirms, "If for the sake of Christ and righteousness, we are accounted as the scorn and off-scouring of all things . . . and have all manner of evil spoken of us falsely, it must not seem strange or unexpected to us . . . but we must bear it patiently, and exceedingly rejoice in hope of our reward in heaven."[2] Paul says, "We have become, and are still, like the scum of the world, the refuse of all things" (1 Cor. 4:13). Scum? Refuse? Really? That seems a little over the top until we recognize that extreme repugnance lurking at the heart of contempt.

Have you ever experienced anything like this? Have you ever been the object of scorn—silent disdain, open hostility, fierce opposition, scathing ridicule, cutting criticism? What about in the classroom? Perhaps one of your professors thinks it's open season on the Christian faith, blaming it for every imaginable evil under the sun. What about in the workplace? Perhaps some of your colleagues are suspicious of Christianity. Their conversations alienate you; their interests and attitudes are antithetical to the faith you hold dear. What about in the home? Is your spouse or sibling a source of opposition? He scorns you for your desire to follow Christ. She scorns you for your desire to speak of Christ. Have you ever been the object of this kind of ridicule?

I don't want to sound like an alarmist, but I believe Christians in the West are on the cusp of entering an age when our society will generally hold us in contempt. Gradually, our position on every ethical issue is being labeled *hate*: to speak out against sin is *hate*; to challenge those who continue obstinately in their sin is *hate*; to support life is to *hate* women; and to support marriage is to *hate* homosexuals. The issue surrounding homosexuality is particularly disconcerting because the debate is increasingly framed in categories such as tolerance versus intolerance, enlightenment versus ignorance, and—of course—love versus hate. How do we engage with those who categorize us like this? How do we react as we're increasingly marginalized in the public sphere? How do we handle this kind of opposition?

For an answer, we turn to Psalm 123. This brief psalm consists of two sections: verses 1–3a and verses 3b–4. The term *for* (meaning *because*)—in the middle of verse 3—marks the transition between the two sections. The psalmist prays in the first, and explains why he prays in the second. I'm going to do something a little different; I'm going to begin my analysis of this psalm by looking at the second section first. Why? It will be easier to understand what the psalmist prays if we first understand the reason he is praying. Got it?

## The Reason for the Psalmist's Prayer (vv. 3b–4)

"For we have had more than enough of contempt. Our soul has had more than enough of the scorn of those who are at ease, of the contempt of the proud."

These verses showcase three important details. First, the psalmist speaks in the first person plural: "We have had . . . Our soul has had. . . ." Clearly, he's speaking on behalf of a group of people. Second, the psalmist identifies the cause of their suffering as "scorn" and "contempt." What makes this kind of attack so burdensome? If you've ever been on the receiving end of it, you already know the answer—it's unjust, undeserved, and unreasonable. Third, the psalmist says they've had "more than enough." He actually says it twice. The Hebrew term literally means to be saturated. The psalmist's point, therefore, is that they've endured all they can bear.

Scripture describes numerous instances of this kind of opposition. I think a particularly illuminating example is what the remnant experienced when they returned to Jerusalem after years of captivity in Babylon. Incidentally, some scholars believe this psalm was written during that time period. The British Museum in London owns an artifact known as the Cyrus Cylinder, which provides an account

of Cyrus's conquest of Babylon in 539 BC.[3] Interestingly, it also explains how Cyrus, the king of Persia, returned the images of gods
collected by Babylon during its conquests to their original temples
and how he arranged for the return of displaced people groups to
their native homelands. Among these displaced people were the Jews
Nebuchadnezzar had deported to Babylon after his destruction of
Jerusalem in 586 BC.

According to the Book of Ezra, God stirred the spirit of Cyrus to
issue a decree permitting the Jews to return to Jerusalem to rebuild
the temple (Ezra 1:1). This return fulfilled God's promise that he
would restore a remnant of his people to their land after they spent
seventy years of exile in Babylon (Jeremiah 25:11–12). Upon returning
to Jerusalem, the remnant immediately had to confront "adversaries"
who approached them on seemingly peaceful terms, offering to help
them with their reconstruction project (Ezra 4:1–2). But the remnant
respond pointedly: "You have nothing to do with us in building a
house to our God; but we alone will build to the LORD, the God of
Israel" (Ezra 4:3). Rather than backing down, their adversaries tried
a different strategy, bribing counselors to appear before the king in
an attempt to persuade him to halt work on the temple. Essentially,
these counselors were lobbyists who spread misinformation—false
reports and accusations. As a result of their effort, the remnant's
reconstruction of the temple was halted for a time.

Why were these people so opposed to the remnant of Jews who
were trying to rebuild the temple? Certainly, they were motivated
politically as they wanted to exert control over the region. But there
were religious motivations at play too, because these people were
the descendants of the foreigners that the king of Assyria had trans-
planted into the region more than a century earlier. When their ancestors first arrived in the land, God sent lions to harass them because
they were openly idolatrous. Trying to survive in a hostile place,
the people asked the king to send an Israelite priest to teach them
the customs of the "god" of the land. As a result, "they feared the
LORD but also served their own gods, after the manner of the nations
from among whom they had been carried away" (2 Kings 17:33). In
other words, they mixed the worship of God with the worship of

false gods. That's known as syncretism—blending together various religious beliefs and practices. This false religion lies at the bottom of the open hostility they display toward the remnant of Jews who return from Babylon.

Whenever people confront the true worship of God, they respond either negatively or positively. Neutrality is rare. When the response is negative, God's people who truly worship him can expect to experience opposition. Christ declares, "Blessed are those who are persecuted for righteousness' sake, for theirs is the kingdom of heaven" (Matthew 5:10). Do you remember the immediate context for this declaration? The Beatitudes. So what is Christ saying? He's letting us know that the world admires the self-confident, not the poor in spirit; it admires the lighthearted, not the sorrowful; it admires the proud, not the meek; it admires the shameless, not the righteous; it admires the avenger, not the merciful; it admires the self-indulgent, not the pure in heart; and it admires the aggressor, not the peacemaker. In short, the world despises Christ and, therefore, all who are united to him.

Let's not pretend otherwise—this kind of opposition makes us weary. At times on our journey homeward, we find ourselves in circumstances similar to those of the psalmist, and we cry out accordingly: "We have had more than enough!" We feel like we've reached the saturation point. The contempt is too great to bear, and the scorn is too painful to endure. What should we do when we don't think we can continue? We must do what the psalmist does: pray.

## The Content of the Psalmist's Prayer (vv. 1–3a)

Having considered why the psalmist is praying, we're now in a better position to make sense of what he is praying, which we will do by answering three questions. Where does he look? How does he look? Why does he look?

## The Object of His Looking (v. 1)

"To you I lift up my eyes, O you who are enthroned in the heavens!"

Interestingly, the psalmist speaks here in the first-person singular. In verses 3b–4, he identifies a problem that plagues God's people as a whole, but he knows the answer to the problem lies in a *personal* application and appropriation of truth. He can't look on behalf of the whole group, and they can't look on his behalf. Each must look to God individually.

Perhaps you've noticed that older couples occasionally exchange glances that can transfer enough information to fill a small treatise. By that, I mean they know what each other is thinking without exchanging words because they read each other's eyes. That's the idea in this verse. When in trouble, we lift up our eyes to God with the assurance that he's intimately acquainted with our every look, squint, frown, tear, and wrinkle. Our eyes speak volumes, and he misses nothing. "We need not speak in prayer," says Charles Spurgeon, "for a glance of the eye will do it all."[4]

As the psalmist lifts up his eyes, he focuses on a singular truth: God is "enthroned in the heavens." In what sense is God in heaven? Does his enthronement in heaven mean he isn't present elsewhere? No. As Thomas Watson explains, "God is said to be in heaven, not because he is so included there as if he were nowhere else; for 'the highest heaven' cannot contain him (1 Kings 8:27). But the meaning is that he is chiefly resident in what the apostle calls 'the third heaven,' where he reveals his glory most to saints and angels (2 Corinthians 12:2)."[5] Now, why does the psalmist emphasize God's throne in heaven? According to John Calvin, the psalmist is making the point that—when opposition abounds—we must remember that God's power remains in heaven in "infinite perfection."[6] In other words, we must focus on the reality that God's sovereign rule over all things is unhindered, unimpaired, and unchallenged. *See Travel Tip #4.* This means that we're never in the grip of blind forces; rather, everything that happens to us is divinely planned and orchestrated, including, says George Swinnock, "all things, not only our comforts, but also our crosses; not only the love of God, but also the *hatred of the world*, and the malice of hell."[7] When we're the object of scorn and contempt, therefore, we look to God who's enthroned in the heavens, governing all things.

## The Manner of His Looking (v. 2)

"Behold, as the eyes of servants look to the hand of their master, as the eyes of a maidservant to the hand of her mistress, so our eyes look to the LORD our God, till he has mercy on us."

In this verse, the psalmist uses a moving analogy. He says he looks to God as a humble servant looks to his master or her mistress. That's somewhat difficult for us to grasp, because we no longer live in the world of masters and servants. We have some idea of the significance of this relationship from reading books and watching movies, but we have no personal experience. The psalmist is describing a relationship in which one person does the bidding of another—a relationship in which one person looks to another for support, guidance, and protection.

If a servant meets with opposition in the performance of his duty, what does he do? He has no choice but to refer the matter to his master. He looks to his master to deal with it as he deems best. What would it have been like to be a servant in the psalmist's day? No rights. No means of defense. No process of appeal. Servants were victims of all sorts of abuse, and their only recourse was to seek their master's protection. That's the word picture in this verse. The psalmist is looking to God the way a helpless servant looks to his master.

## The Focus of His Looking (v. 3)

"Have mercy upon us, O LORD, have mercy upon us."

This is the psalmist's expectation as he looks: God will have mercy and will assist him in his plight. Similarly, when we experience opposition, we can be certain that God will have mercy upon us. Now, this mercy may come in one of two ways: God will either remove us from trouble or he will support us in trouble. Understanding this point is absolutely crucial: God doesn't always remove us from a bad situation, but he always supports us. How? Through his Word, he revives our sense of his distinguishing love.

He's the King of kings, the Lord of lords, the blessed and glorious Sovereign (1 Timothy 6:15). He's the high and lofty One who inhabits eternity—to whom millions of years are but a moment.

He's boundless in his being, omnipotent in his power, unsearchable in his wisdom, and inconceivable in his goodness. Before him, angels (the highest of creatures) veil their faces. The whole creation is less than nothing in comparison to him. Wonder of wonders: Christ died to bring us to this God. Knowing Christ is the difference between everything and nothing; feast and famine; fullness and emptiness; a refreshing oasis and a crippling desert; heaven and hell; an eternity of joy and an eternity of sorrow. God has mercy upon us, strengthening us in the midst of trouble by warming our faith beside the fire of his love in Christ.

## Conclusion

It's extremely important that we start looking this way when we face opposition, because it guards us against one of the most potent threats to our spiritual well-being—bitterness. When we suffer unjustly, undeservedly, and unreasonably, we're prone to fits of anger, feelings of resentment, and longings for revenge. This spirit of bitterness is a source of great spiritual peril because it permeates and cripples the soul.

Bitterness functions a lot like mercury. Metallic mercury evaporates when exposed to the air, and even a few drops can cause contamination. When a human breathes in the contaminated air, the mercury impairs vision and speech; upsets balance and coordination; damages the heart, lungs, and kidneys; and attacks the immune system. In January 2004, a student brought a quarter cup of mercury to a middle school in Gardnerville, Nevada. It contaminated buses and classrooms, and the clothing of over fifty children, and forced the state to spend nearly $100,000 to decontaminate the school.[8]

That's what bitterness does. It contaminates everything—it distorts, impairs, weakens, exhausts, and torments. When we're victims of scorn and contempt, bitterness poses a great danger. But when we look to God, we can see that opposition isn't ultimately about us, but him. As servants, we look to our Master, trusting in his providence, hoping in his goodness, and resting in his justice. We lift our gaze reverently, obediently, expectantly, submissively, continuously, confidently, and patiently. "So our eyes look to the LORD our God, till he has mercy upon us." God has his times and his seasons, and we wait for him while looking to the One who's enthroned in the heavens—"a place of prospect and a place of power."[9]

## Questions

1. Why is the world opposed to Christ?
2. Opposition makes us vulnerable to sin. Give examples.
3. How does the psalmist cope with opposition?
4. What does it mean to look to God?
5. Why is resting in God's sovereignty essential to enduring through opposition?
6. Are you struggling with opposition? If so, how are you handling it?
7. Are you vulnerable to any particular temptation?
8. How can you turn this psalm into a prayer? List specific requests.

# 5

# Facing Danger

## *Psalm 124*

[1] If it had not been the LORD who was on our side—let Israel now say—
[2] if it had not been the LORD who was on our side when people rose up against us,
[3] then they would have swallowed us up alive, when their anger was kindled against us;
[4] then the flood would have swept us away, the torrent would have gone over us;
[5] then over us would have gone the raging waters.
[6] Blessed be the LORD, who has not given us as prey to their teeth!
[7] We have escaped like a bird from the snare of the fowlers;
the snare is broken, and we have escaped!
[8] Our help is in the name of the LORD, who made heaven and earth.

Have you ever missed something that was blatantly obvious?

Sherlock Holmes and Dr. Watson were camping in a tent. Holmes woke up Watson in the middle of the night and pointed up at the stars. Watson blinked the sleep from his eyes as Holmes asked what he deduced.

Watson said, "Well, astronomically, I deduce there are millions of galaxies and potentially billions of planets. Astrologically, I deduce that Saturn is in Leo. Meteorologically, I deduce that we will have a beautiful day tomorrow. What about you, Holmes, what do you deduce?"

"Watson," said Holmes slowly, "I deduce that someone has stolen our tent."[1]

Some of us can relate to Dr. Watson—a little too well, perhaps, particularly when it comes to learning from the past. Although there are obvious lessons to be learned from every epoch of history, we're often unaware of them because most of us possess a natural aversion to the subject. This is true even within Christian circles where having a sense of history—especially our biblical and ecclesiastical family history—is one of our most pressing needs. Why? Because remembering the past is pivotal to living well in the present.

The Israelites likely sang Psalm 124 on their way to Jerusalem to celebrate one of their annual festivals commemorating a specific event in their national history—an event that informed their world view, framed their perspective, and shaped their identity. We need that kind of appreciation for our own history.

So how are we going to approach this psalm? We're going to focus on David's three references to "the LORD" (vv. 1, 6, 8).

### The Greatness of Their Danger (vv. 1–5)

"If it had not been the LORD who was on our side—"

One of my fondest childhood memories is playing street hockey—a great Canadian tradition. Each day after school, no matter the weather, a dozen or so of us gathered on the lightly-trafficked street in front of our homes to play. These games lasted until dark—or until our moms called us in for supper. The games were filled with Sherwood sticks, multicolored jerseys, freezing temperatures, sweaty hats and gloves, road-worn goalie pads, bloodied knees, bruised elbows, and—of course—boyhood dreams of playing in the NHL. One of the regulars had an older brother, Jeff, who always got home from school later than the rest of us, and so always joined the team that was losing when he arrived. It didn't matter what the score was when he got there; with Jeff on their side, the previously losing team always staged a remarkable comeback. Why? Jeff stood head and shoulders above the rest of us, and he could score from anywhere on the street. His slap shot was the envy of every boy in the neighborhood. Inevitably, Jeff's team won.

When we magnify that scenario by a billion, we begin to come close to what David celebrates in this psalm. Twice, he declares that God was on their side (vv. 1–2) and so their deliverance was never in question because omnipotence was working for them. He drives his point home by exhorting the people to imagine what it would have been like if God had *not* been on their side when their enemies "rose up" against them (v. 2) and paints two word pictures to describe what would have happened. First, "they would have swallowed us up alive, when their anger was kindled against us" (v. 3). Here, David compares their enemies to an earthquake—the ground shakes, cracks, and opens, swallowing up everything beneath it. Second, "the flood would have swept us away, the torrent would have gone over us; then over us would have gone the raging waters" (vv. 4–5). Here, David compares their enemies to a flood—the river swells, breaks over its banks, and sweeps away everything in its path.

Both word pictures convey absolute desolation. They speak of something sudden, violent, overwhelming, uncontrollable, inescapable, powerful, and terrifying. David wants to make sure the people see his point: if God had not been on their side, their enemies would have utterly destroyed them.

## The Greatness of Their Deliverance (vv. 6–7)

"Blessed be the LORD, who has not given us as prey to their teeth! We have escaped like a bird from the snare of the fowlers; the snare is broken, and we have escaped!"

David attributes their deliverance to divine intervention and again creates two word pictures to make his point. First, he speaks of a lamb escaping from a lion's mouth (v. 6). On occasion, I watch nature programs on television, and I particularly enjoy watching anything about lions or leopards. I can't look away once the carnage begins: the lioness tackling her prey, biting down on its neck to strangle it. She stands there, panting, with the helpless animal dangling from her mouth, waiting patiently—and confidently—for her prey to breathe its last so that the pride can begin to feed. Lambs do not escape from a lion's mouth.

Second, David speaks of a bird escaping from a fowler's snare (v. 7). This word picture is perhaps a little foreign to us, but he's describing a bird caught in a net. Let me attempt to update the image just a little. Three well-camouflaged men are hiding in a grove of trees. A dove flies directly at them. It's within twenty feet, and closing fast. There are three twelve-gauge shotguns aimed at the dove. In a word, it's over; the dove has no escape route.

Both word pictures convey a sense of overwhelming helplessness. The lamb can't free itself from the jaws of the lioness. The bird can't free itself from the fowler's net. Similarly, David and his people are in a position of great danger and utter helplessness. But what happens? God intervenes miraculously.

Now, what event did David have in mind when he wrote this psalm? We have no idea, because he doesn't see fit to tell us. Perhaps he's thinking of the time when Goliath taunted the army of Israel (1 Samuel 17). Goliath—an enormous man—challenged the Israelites to send out a champion to fight against him, but they were "dismayed and greatly afraid" (v. 11). The Israelites recognized the danger and knew they were overmatched. But when David arrives on the scene, he quickly volunteers for giant-to-man combat. Do you remember Goliath's boast, upon seeing David? "Come to me," he said, "and I will give your flesh to the birds of the air and to the beasts of the field" (v. 44). David simply responds, "I come to you in the name of the LORD of hosts. . . . This day the LORD will deliver you into my hand" (vv. 45–46). And he did.

Or, perhaps David's thinking of one of the close calls he had during the years when Saul was hunting him (1 Samuel 23). One time, when David and his men were hiding in the wilderness of Maon, they were on one side of a hill, while Saul and his army were on the other. Everyone knew it was just a matter of time before Saul would overtake David. He was literally closing in for the kill; the situation was hopeless. Suddenly, a messenger arrived at Saul's camp: "Hurry and come, for the Philistines have made a raid against the land"

(v. 27). Saul left. Acknowledging God's miraculous intervention, David named the place "the Rock of Escape" (v. 28).

Or, perhaps David is thinking of the occasion when his son Absalom decided the time was ripe for a coup and descended upon Jerusalem (2 Samuel 15). David fled out the back door. The situation was devastating, and David's doom seemed certain. Ahithophel counseled Absalom to pursue his father without a moment's hesitation, advising him to strike immediately before David had time to rally his supporters and stage a counterattack (2 Samuel 17). But Hushai, who was secretly working for David, contradicted Ahithophel's counsel, advising Absalom to wait until he had solidified his own position. The delay proved disastrous: "The LORD had ordained to defeat the good counsel of Ahithophel, so that the LORD might bring harm upon Absalom" (v. 14).

In each of these instances, David and his people were on the verge of certain destruction. The earth was about to swallow them up, and the water was about to sweep them away. They were like a lamb dangling from a lion's mouth, and a bird languishing in a fowler's snare. Facing great danger, they experience great deliverance. Why? They belong to a great God.

## The Greatness of Their God (v. 8)

"Our help is in the name of the LORD, who made heaven and earth."

In this verse, David celebrates God's work of creation. Do his words sound familiar? They should, since we heard them in Psalm 121:2: "My help comes from the LORD, who made heaven and earth." Why does this truth seem so appealing to David? I think it's because it speaks of God's almighty power. Stephen Charnock describes God's power as "that ability and strength whereby he can bring to pass whatsoever he please, whatsoever his infinite wisdom can direct, and whatsoever the infinite purity of his will can resolve."[2] God's omnipotence is evident in creation's immensity, complexity, diversity, and beauty. "By the word of the LORD the heavens were made, and by the breath of his mouth all their host" (Psalm 33:6). This great truth led Isaac Watts to pen these tremendous words:

I sing the mighty pow'r of God, that made the mountains rise,
That spread the flowing seas abroad, and built the lofty skies.
I sing the wisdom that ordained the sun to rule the day;
The moon shines full at his command, and all the stars obey.[3]

David brings the people to the point where they can declare: "our help is in the name of the LORD." How does he do it? He reminds them of God's past deliverance and shows them how to apply their knowledge of God's past deliverance to their present circumstances. That's why he begins the psalm the way he does: "If it had not been the LORD who was on our side—Let Israel *now say*—if it had not been the LORD who was on our side." His exhortation is in the present tense, because he wants his fellow countrymen to make history a present reality. He wants them to take to heart the obvious. He wants them to be convinced of God's great deliverance in the past so that it shapes their thinking in the present and allows them to look ahead into the future and declare with unshakeable confidence: "our help is in the name of the LORD."

## Conclusion

At one time, the earth was about to swallow us up, and the water was about to sweep us away. We were like a lamb dangling from a lion's mouth, and a bird languishing in a fowler's snare. Interestingly, New Testament writers employ each of these word pictures to describe Satan (Matthew 10:16; John 10:12; 2 Corinthians 11:3; 1 Peter 5:8; Revelation 12:15). Because of our sin, we were in bondage to Satan. Our predicament was hopeless. But here's a precious truth: God "was on our side." I wonder if Paul had these words in mind when he wrote: "If God is for us, who can be against us?" (Romans 8:31). *See Travel Tip #1.* Paul celebrates a number of things in this verse.

First, he celebrates our *past deliverance*: "He who did not spare his own Son, but gave him up for us all . . ." (Romans 8:32). When Christ died for us, God didn't withhold one drop of his wrath. That is to say, there was no mercy. R. C. Sproul observes:

The fullest manifestation of the curse is found in Jesus' cry from the cross about being forsaken. To be cursed of God is to be forsaken by God. Jesus' cry was not merely an expression of disillusionment or an imagined sense of forsakenness. For him to complete his work of redemption, he actually had to be forsaken. He had to bear the curse of the Father in his own person. The Father had to turn his back on his only begotten Son. The Father had to cover his face and not let Jesus see the light of his countenance.[4]

For Christ to be a curse, he had to bear the full measure of the curse—including hell itself. At the time of his greatest distress, his Father didn't spare him. God heard Naaman when he cried for healing; he heard Hannah when she cried for a child; he heard Hagar when she cried for help; he heard the Ninevites when they cried for mercy; he heard Elijah when he cried for deliverance. Yet there's nothing but deafening silence when Christ cries, "My God, my God, why have you forsaken me?" (Matthew 27:46).

Christ doesn't cry out with a loud voice because of what men do to him. They reject, abuse, ridicule, betray, and desert him. But those things never cause him to cry out with a loud voice. Christ cries out with a loud voice because of what his Father does to him. On the cross, Christ is in complete darkness—external and internal—because his Father has forsaken him. Why did Christ need to suffer in this way? The reason is our sin. Christ submitted to the punishment of desertion—that which we deserve for deserting God. "He poured out his soul to death and was numbered with the transgressors" (Isaiah 53:12). He did so to atone for our sin—to satisfy God's justice, appease God's wrath, and secure God's mercy.

Secondly, Paul celebrates our *future assurance*: "How will he not also with him graciously give us all things . . ." (Romans 8:32). If God didn't spare his own Son, but gave him up for us all, then surely he won't withhold anything from us. To put it another way, if the purchasing price of our salvation is the blood of God's own Son, then surely we'll receive the inheritance. "In giving his Son," notes John Stott, "[God] gave everything. The cross is the guarantee of the continuing, unfailing generosity of God."[5] If God delivered us from the wages of sin, the torments of hell, and the clutches of Satan—through the sacrifice of his Son—he will see us through to the end. It isn't our faith in Christ that saves us, or our hold on Christ that saves us, or our joy in Christ that saves us, or our hope in Christ that saves us. It's the merit of Christ that saves us.

Finally, Paul celebrates our *present confidence*: "If God is for us, who can be against us?" (Romans 8:31). From start to finish, Scripture is emphatic: there's no opposition to God. He saves us and preserves us. Mark it: he hasn't promised us immunity from distress, danger, or difficulty, nor has he promised us immunity from great pain, great loss, or great sorrow. But he *has* promised that nothing can separate us from his love and that nothing can alter his plan for us. This realization imparts spiritual fortitude as we journey home. Looking back, we behold a great God delivering us from a great danger. We live at present in the light of that great deliverance, celebrating the wonderful truth that "our help is in the name of the LORD."

## Questions

1. What do you fear? What keeps you awake at night?
2. Do you feel trapped? If so, why?
3. How has God delivered you in the past?
4. How has God promised to deliver you in the future?
5. What's the relationship between the past, present, and future in the Christian's experience?
6. What does God's power mean for your present circumstances?
7. How can you turn this psalm into a prayer? List specific requests.

# 6

# Finding Security

## *Psalm 125*

[1] Those who trust in the LORD are like Mount Zion, which cannot be moved, but abides forever.

[2] As the mountains surround Jerusalem, so the LORD surrounds his people, from this time forth and forevermore.

[3] For the scepter of wickedness shall not rest on the land allotted to the righteous, lest the righteous stretch out their hands to do wrong.

[4] Do good, O LORD, to those who are good, and to those who are upright in their hearts!

[5] But those who turn aside to their crooked ways the LORD will lead away with evildoers! Peace be upon Israel!

Let's imagine I live in Malaysia. Ethnically, I'm Malay, and that means I'm Muslim. I have no choice in the matter—to be Malay is to be Muslim. It's the law. The Malays comprise ninety percent of the country's population, while people of Chinese and Indian descent make up most of the rest. Among these there are a number of Christians. I often drive by a small evangelical church in my neighborhood, and one of my colleagues at the office where I work is a Christian. I decide to purchase a Bible and start reading it. God convicts me of my sin and shows me my need of a Savior. The wind blows where it wishes, and I'm born again. I repent and believe in Christ. What happens next? I've just broken the law—the punishment for which is imprisonment. I have a wife and children to think about. What's going to happen to me? I can't worship down the street at the evangelical church because if I attend there, the police might charge those Christians with proselytizing a Muslim. How am I going to live in these conditions?

Now, let's imagine a completely different scenario. I live in America. I'm a fifth-generation Christian. My ancestors have experienced the privilege of living in a country founded upon biblical principles. Of late, however, two powerful forces have merged in my society.[1] The first is "moral myopia." Myopia is the technical term for shortsightedness. For those who are shortsighted, everything beyond a certain distance looks fuzzy. That's my society. Most people can't see the future ramifications of today's moral relativism. The second force is "an aggressive agenda of absolute conformity." In other words, my society expects everyone to subscribe to its standard of morality—or lack thereof. Because these two forces have merged the message I'm getting is this: I must embrace an "ethic of sexual anarchy bounded only by the principle of consent." If I don't, I'll be dismissed as the moral equivalent of a racist. I see this being applied to everything from the Boy Scouts of America to the Winter Olympics in Russia. The idea is being pushed politically and legislatively. It's being pushed in the educational system. And it's being pushed by just about every facet of the media.

To varying degrees, both of these scenarios are examples of living under what the psalmist calls "the scepter of wickedness" (v. 3). The term "scepter" points to political power. Evidently, the psalmist is writing at a time when Israel is under the rule of a wicked king—perhaps even a foreign king. Not surprisingly, wickedness is beginning to permeate society. As a result, it's becoming increasingly difficult to live as one of God's people. The psalmist is concerned that this wickedness will corrupt the righteous—perhaps they'll "stretch out their hands to do wrong" (v. 3). The situation is disturbing, disconcerting, and disheartening.

That's what the psalmist is experiencing as he writes, but he sees his way through the darkness by focusing on three certainties.

## The Certainty of God's Protection (vv. 1–3)

"Those who trust in the LORD are like Mount Zion, which car not be moved, but abides forever. As the mountains surround Jeru salem, so the LORD surrounds his people, from this time forth an forevermore. For the scepter of wickedness shall not rest on the lan allotted to the righteous, lest the righteous stretch out their hand to do wrong."

What does it mean to "trust in the LORD"? We answered tha question back in Psalm 121:2, "My help comes from the LORD, wh made heaven and earth." We answered it again in Psalm 124:8, "Ou help is in the name of the LORD, who made heaven and earth." I summary, to trust in God is to rest in who he is. *See Travel Tip #* We rest in his wisdom. He knows all things by one infinite act o understanding and he orchestrates all things to achieve the best en through the best means. To trust in God is to rest in his power. He enthroned in the heavens and his rule is unchallenged and unhin dered. To trust in God is to rest in his goodness. He has taken us t himself as his children and he's a compassionate Father who want what's best for us.

How does God relate to those who trust him? First, he strengthen them. The psalmist says they're "like Mount Zion, which cannot b moved, but abides forever" (v. 1). Some people are like the sand— unstable. Some are like the wind—unpredictable. And some are lik the sea—unsteady. But God's people are like Mount Zion—the rock which served as the original fortifications for the city of Jerusalem It speaks of stability and immovability. God makes us like Moun Zion by granting us spiritual fortitude to stand in the face of sys temic wickedness.

Second, God surrounds those who trust him. The psalmist says tha God surrounds his people "as the mountains surround Jerusalem' (v. 2). Historically, mountains have served as natural fortifications We can't understand, for example, the history between Spain and Portugal or England and Scotland, without taking into consideratior the terrain dividing these nations. The psalmist's point is that Goc surrounds his people like a mountain range—he provides protec tion. In September 2011, my family and I had the opportunity to visit the Great Wall of China. It's a magnificent sight—thousands of miles long, thirty feet high, and eighteen feet wide. Apparently, it was originally constructed to keep out the Mongols and other nomadic invaders, but it has been breached on several occasions over the centuries. Do you know how? The invaders simply bribed the gatekeepers.[2] Any man-made wall is penetrable, but nothing penetrates God's wall.

Now, if it's true that God strengthens and surrounds those who trust him, then why is it that many of his people suffer under "the scepter of wickedness"? Stated another way, why do so many of his people experience opposition and persecution? This question perplexes a lot of people, but needlessly so. God's commitment to strengthen and surround his people isn't a promise to give them a life of ease—unhindered and undisturbed. God never promises his people any such thing. He never promises us that we'll pass through life untouched and unscathed by the negative effects of the fall.

For many years, I struggled with the story of Jonathan. In 1 Samuel 14, we read that the Philistines assemble an army, and send out raiding parties. The Israelites don't possess any iron weapons, so they're hiding in caves and cisterns. Their king, Saul, is also hiding in a cave, his army having dwindled to six hundred men. Ahijah, a descendant of Eli, is with Saul. Here we have a rejected priest and a rejected king huddled together in a cave, cowering before the enemy. Thankfully, there's still a man who thinks great thoughts of God: Saul's son Jonathan.

The story is really a study in contrasts. Saul hides himself, while Jonathan shows himself. Saul stays back, while Jonathan crosses over. Saul lies low, while Jonathan climbs up. Saul avoids the enemy, while Jonathan engages the enemy. Saul looks to himself, while Jonathan looks to God. The key to the whole narrative is Jonathan's declaration: "It may be that the LORD will work for us, for nothing can hinder the LORD from saving by many or by few" (1 Samuel 14:6). In this statement and in his actions, Jonathan celebrates God's power. For him, the Philistines' military superiority means nothing; the Israelites' numerical disadvantage means nothing; and the impenetrable rocky terrain means nothing. These obstacles melt like wax in a hot summer sun before the reality that "nothing can hinder the LORD from saving by many or by few." Jonathan and his armor-bearer proceed to attack the Philistine garrison, and God grants them a resounding victory.

If we didn't know the biblical story of Saul and Jonathan, we would likely assume that Jonathan would be the next king of Israel. After all, that's the way it should be. He's one of the good guys. He's a pillar of faith. He's a man of God. Yet here's the harsh reality: Jonathan will be passed over for another (David), mistreated by his father, and killed by the Philistines on a lonely hill. Some of us struggle with Jonathan's fate. Why? Deep down, we think obedience merits reward. Because we follow God, we think he should use his boundless power to ensure that our lives are free of suffering. Let's be honest—none of us struggle with the second part of Jonathan's statement: "nothing can hinder the LORD from saving by many or by few." But most of us struggle with the first part of his statement: "It may be that the LORD will work for us."

God doesn't promise his people a life of ease. He promises to strengthen and surround those who trust him, thereby protecting them from *ultimate* evil. *See Travel Tip #3.* What precisely does this mean? John Owen explains, "Those whom the Lord will certainly preserve forever in the state and condition of trusting in him, they shall never be forsaken of him nor separated from him."[3] As discussed in Chapter 2, there's something far worse than temporal suffering. There's something worse than losing our jobs, health, money, reputation, or even our lives.

What's the loss of these things in comparison to losing God? If he's infinite, then the loss of him must be infinite. If he's incomprehensible, then the loss of him must be incomprehensible. Conversely, if he's infinite, then the gain of him must be infinite. If he's incomprehensible, then the gain of him must be incomprehensible. God strengthens and surrounds his people by preserving them for "what no eye has seen, nor ear heard, nor the heart of man imagined, what [he] has prepared for those who love him" (1 Corinthians 2:9).

Prevailing conditions will sorely test us, tempting us to succumb to frustration, disillusionment, bitterness, and impatience. These, in turn, might tempt us to "stretch out [our] hands to do wrong." But here's the promise: "the scepter of wickedness shall not rest on the land." That is to say, God will limit the extent and impact of this wickedness. He will restrain it because he's mindful of our frailty and vulnerability. And he will keep us ultimately for "a salvation ready to be revealed in the last time" (1 Peter 1:5).

## The Certainty of God's Provision (v. 4)

"Do good, O LORD, to those who are good, and to those who are upright in their hearts!"

Upon hearing the term "good," most of us immediately think in terms of minimal suffering, financial security, fulfilled dreams, and resolved problems. Why? Far too often, we define *good* according to what we want instead of what we need, what makes us happy instead of what makes us holy, what's visible instead of what's invisible, and what's temporal instead of what's eternal. In a word, we define *good* according to the interest of the flesh rather than the welfare of the soul. But God's chief purpose isn't to fulfill our dreams, nor is it to make us healthy and wealthy. His chief purpose is to glorify himself by conforming us to the image of his Son (Romans 8:28–30). "God's primary goal," says Paul Tripp, "is not changing our situations and relationships so that we can be happy, but changing us through our situations and relationships so that we will be holy."[4]

That's the "good," which the psalmist has in view in this verse. He asks that God accomplish his purpose (that which is good) through the very circumstances that threaten his people—even as they struggle under "the scepter of wickedness." Suffering tempts us to retreat into a world of self-preoccupation. It tempts us to succumb to what some people call "sovereign stoicism," whereby we resign ourselves to the fact that we must simply perform our duty while bearing whatever comes our way. It also tempts us to succumb to unbridled hysteria, whereby we implode emotionally. To guard against these temptations, we must remember that there's no greater pledge of God's love for us than his desire to make us holy (Ephesians 5:25–27). He has our long-term good in view. He desires to increase our faith, hope, and love, to purge us of sin, to wean our hearts from this world, to make us more compassionate toward others, and to cause us to love him above all else. Affliction might assail us, but it can never destroy us. Indeed, God has designed it as part of the process by which he sanctifies us. And this is *good*.

### The Certainty of God's Preservation (v. 5)

"But those who turn aside to their crooked ways the LORD will lead away with evildoers! Peace be upon Israel!"

Peering down the corridors of time, the psalmist sees a day of reckoning for "evildoers" and "those who turn aside to their crooked ways." What will happen to them? In a word, "the LORD will lead them away." For starters, that means they'll lose whatever is pleasing and satisfying in this life—all that provides a little happiness. They'll lose their possessions, families, and friends. They'll also lose their hopes, comforts, and delights. But far eclipsing these material losses, they'll lose God—the only source of true happiness. This is the loss of all losses. It's a loss that no words can describe—that no mind can conceive. Those whom God will lead away will become the object of his wrath, as he hides his compassion and tenderness. How terrifying will it be to fall into the hands of God with nothing but the soul to bear his infinite anger!

Regrettably, some of us are inoculated against the reality of hell. It doesn't affect us like it should. For over thirty years, I lived within a two-hour drive of Niagara Falls. Apparently, more than twelve million tourists visit Niagara Falls each year. To be honest, I don't know what all the fuss is about. Why's that? Proximity and familiarity have dulled my sense of amazement. Sadly, the same thing can happen to our appreciation of the things of God. We've heard about our sin so many times that it no longer breaks our hearts. We've heard about Christ's atonement so many times that it no longer warms our hearts. We've heard about God's mercy so many times that it no longer melts our hearts. Or, in the present context, we've heard about hell so many times that it no longer overwhelms our hearts. For this reason, John Piper warns:

If I do not believe in my heart these awful truths—believe them so that they are real in my feelings—then the blessed love of God in Christ will scarcely shine at all. The sweetness of the air of redemption will be hardly detectable. The infinite marvel of my new life will be commonplace. The wonder that to me, a child of hell, all things are given for an inheritance will not strike me speechless with trembling humility and lowly gratitude. The whole affair of salvation will seem ho-hum, and my entrance into paradise will seem as a matter of course. When the heart no longer feels the truth of hell, the gospel passes from *good* news to simply news. The intensity of joy is blunted and the heart-spring of love is dried up.[5]

Piper's point is well made: "When the heart no longer feels the truth of hell, the gospel passes from *good* news to simply news." To persevere under "the scepter of wickedness," or to persevere under any trying circumstance, we must understand what God preserves us from. *See Travel Tip #1.* It's the darkness of night that makes the dawn so uplifting; the torment of pain that makes relief so comforting; the cold of winter that makes spring so encouraging; the loneliness of separation that makes reunion so refreshing. Likewise, it's the prospect of hell that makes the promise of glory so overwhelming.

I just mentioned Niagara Falls. There are two ways to see the falls. You can stand at the railing and see the falls from above—the water rushing over the escarpment, the mist rising in the sky, the noise thundering in your ears, and the spray moistening your face. Or, you can stand in a boat (e.g., the Maid of the Mist), and see the falls from below—the churning water, the deafening noise, the blinding cloud, and the shrieking tourist to your left. Similarly, there are two ways to view the gospel. We view it from below to see its personal significance—what it means for the individual. And we view it from above to see its universal significance—what it means for the cosmos.

When we look from above, we see that the gospel is the good news that God has reconciled "all things" to himself (Colossians 1:20). He has inaugurated a new creation, which awaits its full and final purging from sin. When we look from below, we see that the gospel is the good news that God has reconciled us to himself (Colossians 1:21–22). We were formerly alienated, marked by hostile thoughts and evil deeds (Colossians 1:21). But God has moved us from a position of hostility to a position of peace by removing the barrier to peace—our sin. Now, we rejoice in the fact that Christ "hides our unrighteousness with his righteousness, covers our disobedience with his obedience, and shadows our death with his death, so that the wrath of God cannot find us."[6] We're certain of God's preservation of us from the wrath to come. This heightens "the intensity of joy," feeds "the heart-spring of love," and enables us to see our way ahead when under "the scepter of wickedness."

## Conclusion

These three certainties provide much-needed perspective when we find ourselves living under "the scepter of wickedness." They remind us that God Triune is engaged for our salvation, protection, preservation, and glorification. "On the Father's part, there's sovereign grace and infinite power," according to Thomas Manton. "On the Son's part, there's sufficient merit and eternal intercession. On the Spirit's part, there's continual influence."[7] This God is the ground of our ultimate security.

## Questions

1. What does it mean to trust God?

2. How does God promise to strengthen you?

3. How does God promise to surround you?

4. What is good? What's God's purpose for us? See Rom. 8:28–30.

5. How does God achieve this purpose?

6. What has God preserved (saved) you from?

7. How does this psalm shape your perspective?

8. How can you turn this psalm into a prayer? List specific requests.

# 7

# Experiencing Joy

## *Psalm 126*

[1] When the LORD restored the fortunes of Zion, we were like those who dream.
[2] Then our mouth was filled with laughter, and our tongue with shouts of joy;
then they said among the nations, "The LORD has done great things for them."
[3] The LORD has done great things for us; we are glad.
[4] Restore our fortunes, O LORD, like streams in the Negeb!
[5] Those who sow in tears shall reap with shouts of joy!
[6] He who goes out weeping, bearing the seed for sowing,
shall come home with shouts of joy, bringing his sheaves with him.

"Rejoice always!" (1 Thessalonians 5:16). Personally, I find that to be one of the most difficult commands in all of Scripture to obey. Why? The joy of sense is in present things, whereas the joy of faith is in future things; the joy of sense is in the good of the body, whereas the joy of faith is in the good of the soul; the joy of sense is governed by circumstances, whereas the joy of faith is governed by promises; and the joy of sense rests in the world, whereas the joy of faith rests in God.[1] So what's my point? It's far easier to live by sense than by faith, and that means my joy is often *earthly* rather than *heavenly*— *material* rather than *spiritual*. Consider the following story:

Several years ago, while preaching in the United States, I stayed in the home of a very successful young couple who were surrounded with the trappings of success and growing wealthier by the day. They were enthusiastic members of a church which majored in an effervescent approach to all its activities, and my hosts seemed to be on a permanent "high."

As the husband started the car before leaving for church one night, we heard a startled squeal from under the hood. When he opened it up, their pet cat was sitting there, looking decidedly frightened and minus several patches of fur. Instantly, my hosts surrendered to a frenzied panic, and all their confidence and cheerfulness vanished. Frankly, they were in worse shape than the cat! It took several hours before they recovered.

The whole incident was a bizarre illustration of how flimsy and fragile happiness can be when it is divorced from true blessedness and from the truth of Thomas Watson's assertion that "Blessedness does not lie in externals."[2]

We must learn that true happiness doesn't flow from temporal and material circumstances, but from eternal and spiritual realities. And that's the central theme of Psalm 126. At the outset, I want you to notice three important details. First, there are two principal sections: verses 1–3 and verses 4–6. It's easy to identify them because each begins with a reference to "fortunes" (vv. 1, 4). Second, the term "fortune" isn't a synonym for earthly wealth or treasure, nor is it a synonym for good luck—as in a fortune cookie. The term refers to God's favor. In translating the Hebrew text, both the Authorized Version and New American Standard Version speak of God restoring the captive. That term lets us know that the *fortune* in view is restoration or deliverance. Third, the psalmist looks back in the first section, whereas he looks ahead in the second section.

When we put these three details together, the psalmist's message becomes clear: true joy is fueled by our appreciation of past restoration and our anticipation of future restoration.

### Appreciating Past Restoration (vv. 1–3)

"When the LORD restored the fortunes of Zion . . ."

What's the psalmist talking about? We don't know. One popular theory is that the author is Ezra, and that he penned these words in celebration of the remnant's return from Babylon. That's a very real possibility. But there are plenty of other instances of deliverance in Israel's history. And so, we can't say for certain who the psalmist was or what restoration he has in view, but we do know three of its effects.

## Awe-Inspiring (v. 1)

"When the LORD restored the fortunes of Zion, we were like those who dream."

Some people think they're "living the dream" when they've purchased a classic car or country home, vacationed at some exotic resort, or attained financial freedom (a basic human right, according to what I heard recently from one preacher). James Adams coined the phrase "American Dream" in 1931, describing it as: "each man and each woman shall be able to attain to the fullest stature of which they are innately capable, and be recognized by others for what they are."[3] In our day, many interpret this idea to mean that we should pursue wealth and luxury. As a result, the "American dream" has become synonymous with materialism. Is it possible we're following a brand of American Christianity which embraces a warped notion of the American dream? If so, is it possible we've embraced values that are actually opposed to the Christian faith?

Material prosperity is not what's on the psalmist's mind. When he says that they were "like those who dream," he means that they viewed God's deliverance as too good to be true. It was surprising and overwhelming.

## Joy-Inducing (v. 2)

"Then our mouth was filled with laughter, and our tongue with shouts of joy."

The drastic change in their fortunes was like moving from darkness to light, from life to death. It was a spine-tingling, ear-piercing, knee-slapping, roof-raising time of celebration. True joy isn't about living large or looking good. It's about being delivered. It's about being restored and reconciled to God.

### God-Glorifying (vv. 2–3)

"Then they said among the nations, 'The LORD has done great things for them.' The LORD has done great things for us; we are glad."

As they look on, the nations acknowledge that God has worked powerfully in altering Israel's condition, but they only speak of it as news. They're mere "spectators" of it while God's people are "sharers" in it.[4] At the same time, God's people declare, "The LORD has done great things for us." What makes them great? They're miraculous and marvelous manifestations of his power, unexpected and undeserved manifestations of his grace, and inscrutable and inexplicable manifestations of his wisdom.

### Anticipating Future Restoration (vv. 4–6)

"Restore our fortunes, O LORD . . ."

God has restored their fortunes, yet here the psalmist asks God to restore their fortunes. That seems a little confusing. What's his point? Again, we don't know the writer's specific circumstances. If this psalm indeed describes events following the remnant's return from Babylon, then perhaps the psalmist is expressing his desire for his remaining countrymen to make the journey back to Jerusalem. Whatever the precise circumstances, the people are looking to God to deliver them yet again. The psalmist employs two word pictures to describe their expectation.

### Geographical: From Debilitating Drought to Overflowing Rivers (v. 4)

"Restore our fortunes, O LORD, like streams in the Negeb!"

The Negeb is located in the southern part of Israel, and for much of the year, the wadis (seasonal streams and rivers) are bone dry. I see that sort of thing where I live in Glen Rose, Texas. The Paluxy River runs through the center of town. Often times, it's completely dry by midsummer. It's brown, parched, and cracked. That's how the psalmist feels. He wants God to send rain that will overflow the wadis and soak the land. He knows God's future deliverance will be like a river rushing through a barren land.

**Agricultural: From Sowing in Tears to Reaping with Joy (vv. 5–6)**

"Those who sow in tears shall reap with shouts of joy! He who goes out weeping, bearing the seed for sowing, shall come home with shouts of joy, bringing his sheaves with him."

When a farmer sows his seed in such a harsh climate, he doesn't have much hope. It seems futile. The soil and weather conditions are seemingly against him. But suddenly the rain falls, the seed germinates, the grain grows, and he reaps a tremendous harvest. The psalmist hasn't forgotten God's past restoration. His heart warms whenever he thinks about it. It was awe-inspiring, joy-inducing, and God-glorifying. But things have been tough ever since. He feels like a wadi in the dry season or a farmer sowing seed in the dust. And so, he asks God to restore his fortunes in full confidence that God will answer his prayer. The harvest will come, and his weeping will turn into "shouts of joy."

## Conclusion

When we bring this psalm to this side of the cross, we see that true joy is fueled by our appreciation of past restoration and our anticipation of future restoration. *See Travel Tip #1.* To begin with, we celebrate past restoration. Each of Israel's deliverances (from Egypt to Babylon) point to a far greater deliverance. We were bound under sin's dominion. Imagine the deepest dungeon, darkest cell, thickest chain, and strongest jailer. Got it? You haven't even come close to grasping the depth of our bondage to sin. But Christ has freed us by paying the penalty for our sin.

He canceled the record of debt by nailing it to the cross (Colossians 2:14). When the Romans crucified someone, they fastened the official accusation above the criminal's head: *titulus*. They fixed a *titulus* above Christ's head: the king of the Jews. Well, God the Father also fixed (figuratively speaking) a *titulus* above Christ's head:

the law. God annulled the law when his Son satisfied its demand of perfect obedience and suffered its curse.

Christ has also freed us by breaking the power of our sin. He triumphed over the "rulers and authorities," disarming them and humiliating them (Colossians 2:15). After conquering an enemy, Roman generals would enter the city of Rome with treasures and prisoners in their wake and parade through the city. That's the idea in this verse. At the cross, Christ triumphed over the spiritual powers, putting them to open shame. Satan's rule is twofold: he rules over people by death, and he rules in people by sin. By his death, Christ destroyed both aspects of Satan's rule. He disarmed him.

In Christ, therefore, we breathe the air of freedom. The effect is awe-inspiring, joy-inducing, and God-glorifying. We're like those who dream. Yet, despite our celebration of past deliverance, we're still longing for something. We're waiting for the day when we'll be fully and finally saved. Interestingly, Christ introduces and concludes the Beatitudes with the same promise: "theirs is the kingdom of heaven" (Matthew 5:3, 10). In both instances, the promise is in the present tense. The six intervening promises in the Beatitudes look to the future, indicating that membership in God's kingdom eventually culminates in all of these blessings: we will be comforted, we will inherit the earth, we will be satisfied, we will receive mercy, we will see God, and we will be called the sons of God.[5] These blessings are ours by right—by virtue of our union with Christ and inclusion in his kingdom. But our enjoyment of them now is *partial* and *imperfect*, whereas our enjoyment of them in glory will be *full* and *perfect*.

Until then, we struggle. At times, we feel like a wadi in the dry season. At times, we feel like we're sowing seed in the dust. It's difficult. Are you a dried-up Christian? Do you feel parched and cracked? Are you sowing in tears—confusion, frustration, and disappointment? If so, here are three truths to bear in mind.

First, the dryness doesn't last forever. Those who sow in tears don't do so forever; eventually, they reap with shouts of joy. But here's the thing we must not miss: God chooses when the dry time ends. In this life, we might experience many seasons of abundant rain, or we might experience one long crippling drought. In this life, we might reap a great harvest from our seed sown in tears, or we might not see any harvest. We must not lose sight of the fact that the absolute fulfillment of God's promise is future. *See Travel Tip #3.* We might possess very little during our lifetime, yet we're still blessed because the inheritance belongs to us as members of Christ, who is Lord of all. A day is coming when this "right" will give way to full possession. At Christ's return, we will inherit the new heavens and new earth—the renewed universe from which every remnant of the curse will be removed. At that time, we'll reap with "shouts of joy."

Second, the dryness doesn't change our Father's love for us. Prolonged seasons of drought are particularly troublesome because we often interpret them as signs of God's displeasure. This is a wrong approach. The psalmist cries, "You have kept count of my tossings; put my tears in your bottle. Are they not in your book?" (Psalm 56:8). God is as close to us in the bottom of the valley as on the top of the mountain. He remains with us during the darkest days. We always have his *attention*: "through [Christ] we have access in one Spirit to the Father" (Ephesians 2:18). And we always have his *affection*: he cares for us (1 Peter 5:7). If we wander, he guides us; if we stumble, he holds us; if we fall, he lifts us; if we err, he corrects us; if we grieve, he comforts us. In Christ, we're the object of his eternal love.

Third, the dryness doesn't stifle present joy. When we keep our eyes fixed on past and future deliverance, these spiritual realities transcend all present circumstances. God "has blessed us in Christ with every spiritual blessing in the heavenly places" (Ephesians 1:3). He has reconciled us to himself, poured out his Spirit upon us, made us one with Christ; established us as co-heirs with Christ; and freed us from the bondage of sin and the curse of the law. He grants us free access to himself and calls us his children. And he promises that everything will work together for our good, that nothing will separate us from his love, and that we will inherit his kingdom. That's the cause of true joy.

## Questions

1. Where is true joy found?
2. Do you find it difficult to rejoice? If so, why?

3. What has God delivered you from?

4. What makes you happy? To what extent is your joy contingent on circumstances?

5. How does hope fuel joy?

6. "The dryness doesn't last forever." How does this speak to your present conditions?

7. "The dryness doesn't change our Father's love for us." How does this speak to your present conditions?

8. "The dryness doesn't stifle present joy." How does this speak to your present conditions?

9. How can you turn this psalm into a prayer? List specific requests.

# 8

# Avoiding Worry

## *Psalm 127*

¹ Unless the LORD builds the house, those who build it labor in vain.
Unless the LORD watches over the city, the watchman stays awake in
vain.
² It is in vain that you rise up early and go late to rest, eating the bread
of anxious toil;
for he gives to his beloved sleep.
³ Behold, children are a heritage from the LORD, the fruit of the womb
a reward.
⁴ Like arrows in the hand of a warrior are the children of one's youth.
⁵ Blessed is the man who fills his quiver with them!
He shall not be put to shame when he speaks with his enemies in
the gate.

It consumes. When it grips us, it won't let go; it captivates our
thoughts and overruns our emotions; it dampens our joy and disrupts
our peace. It wraps its tentacles around our souls, tightening its grip
until it saps us of all strength. It keeps us from eating and sleeping.
It prevents us from deriving pleasure from the good gifts God has
so graciously bestowed on us.

It hinders. We aren't much fun to be around when it has us in
its clutches. It strains the relationships between husband and wife,
parent and child, brother and sister. It strains relationships among

believers. On top of that, it makes us so inward-looking that we're useless when it comes to serving others. It puts us on edge. It makes us inattentive, unresponsive, and unsympathetic.

It deceives. It promises to resolve what troubles us and rectify what vexes us. Yet it never contributes one iota to resolving any of our problems. It doesn't give any sound advice, nor does it contribute any deep insight. It doesn't render any peace or comfort. It takes all our time and produces nothing. It takes all our energy and renders nothing. It takes and takes and takes, giving nothing in return.

I'm referring, of course, to *worry*—which someone has described as a "small trickle of fear that meanders through the mind until it cuts a channel into which all other thoughts are drained." Martyn-Lloyd Jones says, "The trouble with the person of little faith is that, instead of controlling his own thought, his thought is being controlled by something else, and, as we put it, he goes round and round in circles. That is the essence of worry."[1]

If you're lying awake for hours every night, I can tell you what you have been doing: you have been going around in circles. You go over the same old miserable details about some person or thing. That is not thought; that is the absence of thought, a failure to think. Something else is controlling and governing your thought, leading to that wretched, unhappy state called worry. As Lloyd-Jones suggests, the only remedy for worry is proper thinking. And that's precisely what we're going to find in Psalm 127. Before diving into the details, we need to do a few things. First, we need to acknowledge what this psalm is *not* about. It's not about solving great theological puzzles, probing the intricacies of complex doctrines, pursuing mountaintop experiences, traversing deep oceans and high peaks to proclaim the gospel to the lost, enduring unspeakable and unthinkable hardships, engaging in great feats of spiritual discipline, attending conferences where thousands sing with one rapturous voice, serving in some cutting-edge ministry, or surrendering all for the kingdom. This psalm is about the ordinary; it's about real life.

Second, we need to identify Solomon's audience. In verse 2, he speaks of God's "beloved." Who's he talking about? Ultimately, God's beloved is Christ, and all who are united to him. "Having loved his own who were in the world, he loved them to the end" (John 13:1). That beautiful statement consists of two parts: Christ loves "his own"—all whom the Father has given to him; and Christ loves "them to the end"—that is, he goes to the cross to bear the penalty for their sin. His love for them is unchanging and unwavering. This ought to be a cause of daily celebration. "We are never nearer Christ," writes John Owen, "than when we find ourselves lost in a holy amazement at his unspeakable love."[2]

Third, we need to recognize the unifying theme of this psalm, which was authored by Solomon. Some people have suggested that Solomon's thought-flow is disjointed or even that it contains two or three unrelated themes. I disagree. Here's the central theme in a single sentence: we have no reason to worry in light of God's all-encompassing providence.

With that said, we're ready for the psalm.

## God's Providence in Providing and Protecting (v. 1)

"Unless the LORD builds the house, those who build it labor in vain. Unless the LORD watches over the city, the watchman stays awake in vain."

Here, Solomon uses two conditional clauses to affirm that all human effort lies prostrate at the throne of God's providence. The first concerns God's *provision*: "Unless the LORD builds the house, those who build it labor in vain." Solomon could be thinking of the temple of God, the city of Jerusalem, or the kingdom of Israel; but it's most likely he's thinking in terms of his actual home. His point is straightforward: the construction of a house is vain apart from God. Why? God is the ultimate cause of all things. The mortar doesn't set, the bricks don't hold, the electricity doesn't work, the edifice doesn't stand, apart from God's providence.

The second conditional clause concerns God's *protection*: "Unless the LORD watches over the city, the watchman stays awake in vain." Solomon knows it's important for the watchman to stay awake. He isn't insinuating that they're free to sleep on the job. But he is pointing out that, even when surrounded by thousands of vigilant watchmen, a city's safety still rests with God. Ultimately, protection comes from him because he's the cause of all things. The most advanced warning system and most sophisticated weaponry won't protect anyone apart from God's providence.

Through these two conditional clauses, Solomon affirms that all human effort lies prostrate before the throne of God's providence. *See Travel Tip #4*. God keeps all things in existence, causes all things to act as they do, and directs all things to their appointed end.

## An Example of God's Providential Provision (v. 2)

"It is in vain that you rise up early and go late to rest, eating the bread of anxious toil; for he gives to his beloved sleep."

This statement seems to relate back to the first conditional clause in verse 1: "Unless the LORD builds the house, those who build it labor in vain." In short, God's providence means we must look to him for provision. In verse 2, Solomon gives a specific example of God's providential provision: the fruit of all our labor is in his hands. Solomon isn't denying the need for hard work; it might be necessary to burn both ends of the candle once in a while, but the key phrase is "anxious toil." He's saying it's pointless to fret and stress needlessly over work. Why? We labor but entrust the results to God. Why? "He gives to his beloved sleep." That's true, and an accurate translation of the Hebrew. But there's another way to translate it: "He gives to his beloved even in his sleep" (New American Standard Version). What does that mean? We need to keep in mind that this psalm was written in an agrarian society, meaning most of its original readers were farmers. Crops are dependent upon the annual cycle of rain and susceptible to pests, storms, and diseases. People can plant, irrigate, and harvest—from sun up to sun down. Ultimately, however, God must cause the seed to grow—he must give while they sleep. Similarly, when it comes to our work, God must give the increase. For this reason, we rest in his providential provision.

## An Example of God's Providential Protection (vv. 3–5)

"Behold, children are a heritage from the LORD, the fruit of the womb a reward. Like arrows in the hand of a warrior are the children of one's youth. Blessed is the man who fills his quiver with them! He shall not be put to shame when he speaks with his enemies in the gate."

This statement relates back to the second conditional clause in verse 1: "Unless the LORD watches over the city, the watchman stays awake in vain." The lesson is that, in light of God's providence, we look to him for protection. But what does this have to do with children? In verse 3, Solomon affirms children are a "heritage" and "reward" from God. In the context, he seems to be saying that they provide a measure of temporal strength, security, and stability. They're "like arrows in the hand of a warrior."

Solomon adds, "Blessed is the man who fills his quiver with them!" I've heard that phrase used many times to encourage couples today to have large families—the larger the better. I've heard it said so many times that it's difficult to imagine this verse could mean anything else. But I don't think the size of a person's family is Solomon's chief point. To get what he's saying, we must enter into his ancient culture. To be old and childless was a harsh existence. There weren't any safety nets or social programs; therefore, as people aged, they became increasingly vulnerable and relied on their children to protect them. Solomon is saying that this protection ultimately comes from God because children come from God. The lesson, therefore, is that we must rest in God's providential protection.

### Conclusion

These are perhaps the two causes of greatest concern in life: provision and protection. According to Solomon, both are in God's hands. When we grasp this, we've entered the realm of proper thinking. We cease to go "round and round in circles" in our mind. We see that anxiety is an exercise in futility.

I want to demonstrate how this plays out in very practical terms. I'm dwelling on this point because *worry* has a stranglehold on far too many of us. Moreover, it has become an acceptable sin, meaning we don't deal with it as we ought. Let's begin by recognizing that there's such a thing as *natural* fear. Examples are always helpful;

so let's suppose I exit the front door of my house and encounter a rattlesnake. (I live in Texas, so this scenario isn't too far-fetched.) Because the snake is venomous and dangerous, I fear it and avoid it. There's nothing wrong with that. As a matter of fact, this kind of fear is essential to human existence; we fear what threatens us, and we avoid what we fear.

But we need to recognize that there's such a thing as *sinful* fear. And so, let's imagine the same scenario: I encounter a rattlesnake outside my house, and I become so afraid that I run back inside the house and decide I'm never going to leave it again. What has just happened? My *natural* fear has become *sinful* fear because I've ascribed *ultimate power* to the object of my fear. It now controls me. Do you see the difference?

Similarly, we need to recognize that there's a difference between *natural* worry and *sinful* worry. Here's another completely hypothetical situation: I own a home on the Gulf Coast. A hurricane is approaching fast, so I board up the windows in my house, make sure my insurance policy is paid, and move my family to safety. There's nothing wrong with that kind of worry. It's sensible and essential to human existence. But imagine a different response to the same scenario. Having done all of the things mentioned above, I then sit around wondering how my life will continue if the storm destroys my house. I begin to distance myself from my wife, and I become irritable with my children. What has happened? My *natural* worry has become *sinful* worry because I've ascribed *ultimate value* to the object of my worry. It now controls me.

Some of us worry about broken relationships, debilitating illnesses, premature death, or financial loss. Some of us worry about failure, rejection, or abandonment. Some of us worry about the state of the world: political structures are wavering, monetary systems are collapsing, and traditional values are disappearing. These things should concern us. But our concerns become *sinful* when they begin to control us. When they control us, it means we fear something more than God. When we fear something more than God, it means we believe there's something greater than God. When we believe there's something greater than God, it means we're guilty of idolatry. As we tear back the layers, we discover that the cause of sinful worry isn't what's happening outside of us but inside of us.

Here are a few more examples to make sure you're getting this point. Let's imagine I fear disease. That's normal. But my fear prevents me from going out in public, and keeps me glued to Google as I self-diagnose every ache and pain. My *natural* fear has become *sinful* fear. I've turned my fear of disease into an idol (*greater in power than God*), whereby it controls me. Or, let's imagine I fear rejection. That's normal. But my fear prevents me from developing relationships, keeps me from communicating with my spouse, or hinders me from displays of affection. My *natural* fear has become *anxious* fear. I've turned my fear of rejection into an idol (*greater in value than God*), whereby it controls me.

This kind of worry is a heart issue, which can only be resolved through the lively application of truth. And that's what Psalm 127 gives us. Solomon celebrates God's all-encompassing providence, demonstrating its reality in two all-important spheres: provision and protection. *See Travel Tip #4.* In light of God's all-encompassing providence, we have no reason to worry. Surely, this is Christ's very point when he declares, "Look at the birds of the air: they neither sow nor reap nor gather into barns, and yet your heavenly Father feeds them. Are you not of more value than they?" (Matthew 6:26). I like to imagine that a flock of sparrows flew overhead when Christ spoke those words. How many sparrows have dotted the skies since creation? Can any of us compute that kind of number? Relatively speaking, they're worthless, yet God watches over them. If God's providence extends to a single sparrow's provision and protection, then surely it extends to his children as well. As Mabel Brown Denison celebrates:

> Of all God's marvels transcendent,
> this wonder of wonders I see,
> that the God of such infinite greatness
> should care for the sparrows—and me.[3]

This "wonder of wonders" calls for faith. Paul writes, "And he put all things under his feet and gave him as head over all things to the church, which is his body, the fullness of him who fills all in all" (Ephesians 1:22–23). All things are subject to Christ. There's his spiritual kingdom whereby he rules by his Spirit and Word in the hearts of his people. There's also his providential kingdom whereby he rules over the world, governing all things. Here's a wonderful truth: Christ rules his providential kingdom for the good of his spiritual kingdom. In other words, God has arranged the world's history in reference to the destiny of his people. "For the eyes of the LORD run to and fro throughout the whole earth, to give strong support to those whose heart is blameless toward him" (2 Chronicles 16:9).

There are no random events, freak accidents, chance encounters, or rogue molecules. His knowledge is perfect: he knows what was, what is, what will be, what can be, and what can't be. He knows all things perfectly, immediately, and distinctly—at every moment. His power is perfect; he has never encountered difficulty—let alone impossibility. "None can stay his hand or say to him, 'What have you done?'" (Daniel 4:35). Every detail of every life was in the mind of God before the foundation of the world. "Wonderful are your works; my soul knows it very well" (Psalm 139:14). We know his goodness dictates his providence, meaning he designs all things for our good. We know his wisdom governs his providence, meaning he knows what's best for us. We know his power accomplishes his providence, meaning he's in ultimate control. Now, that's proper thinking!

> Praise to the Lord, who o'er all things so wondrously reigneth,
> Shelters thee under His wings, yea, so gently sustaineth!
> Hast thou not seen how thy desires e'er have been
> Granted in what He ordaineth?[4]

## Questions

1. What occupies your thoughts? What rules your focus and attention?

2. How does your thinking affect you? Health? Attitude? Relationships? Productivity?

3. "All human effort lies prostrate at the throne of God's providence." Why? What does this mean for your present circumstances?

4. The psalmist contemplates two specific examples of God's providence. What are they? How should this encourage you?

5. What lies at the root of sinful worry?

6. What is the remedy? How does this apply to your current condition?

7. Why does Jesus command us not to worry? See Matt. 6:25–34.

8. How can you turn this psalm into a prayer? List specific requests.

# 9

# Discovering Blessedness

## *Psalm 128*

[1] Blessed is everyone who fears the LORD, who walks in his ways!
[2] You shall eat the fruit of the labor of your hands;
you shall be blessed, and it shall be well with you.
[3] Your wife will be like a fruitful vine within your house;
your children will be like olive shoots around your table.
[4] Behold, thus shall the man be blessed who fears the LORD.
[5] The LORD bless you from Zion!
May you see the prosperity of Jerusalem all the days of your life!
[6] May you see your children's children! Peace be upon Israel!

A couple of decades ago, while working for a relief and development organization, I had the opportunity to visit Haiti. After all these years, one day from that trip still stands out in my memory. At the crack of dawn, I drove from Port-au-Prince into the hills. When the road stopped, I parked the Land Rover and walked two hours up a hill to a community near Bois Joli. My goal was to determine if any of the springs in the area would provide viable sources of drinking water. Survey completed, I set out on the return journey. But I made a huge mistake: I neglected to fill my water bottle in preparation for the two-hour walk back to my vehicle. Thirty minutes later, I realized my folly but—rightly or wrongly—I pressed on. The sun was high over head, and the temperature hovered around 100 degrees. By the time I reached the Land Rover, I was close to passing out. As you can imagine, I had only one thing on my mind—water. It's amazing how trivial everything else seemed by way of comparison.

We live in a world that's unable to satisfy our greatest thirst. Our soul is spiritual; the material can't satisfy it. Our soul is eternal; the temporal can't satisfy it. Our soul is exceptional; the trivial can't satisfy it. Yet what does the world offer? You guessed it: the material, temporal, and trivial. It offers CDs with sounds of loons, whales, oceans, and raindrops. It offers vibrating chairs, massage machines, scented candles, and body-rollers. It offers a host of drugs and medications. It offers innumerable gizmos and gadgets and other mind-numbing distractions. It offers extreme sports, virtual reality, and reality TV. It offers amusements upon amusements. Accompanying all of these offers are promises of happiness, but the world fails to deliver on its promises. It's worse than that, as David Wells explains:

> The American way of life may be the envy of the world, its gadgets and accoutrements sought after and emulated, but the American version of happiness, it turns out, is quite lethal. America is a violent and disturbed country. Its teenagers have the highest suicide rate in the world . . . it leads the world in the consumption of drugs, legal and illegal, in addictions of various kinds, in divorce, in the incidence of depressive illness, and in the marketing of a vast range of therapies to counteract these problems—all of which points to a vast underlying unhappiness.[1]

Looking around, we see that happiness is the focal point of human existence. Parents seek to cultivate it, musicians express it, governments promise it, businesses market it, and commercials sell it. Why? Because people are desperately trying to find it. Yet happiness proves elusive because most people don't know where it's found. As Thomas Watson observes, "Millions of people mistake both the nature of blessedness and the way to it."[2] Why? They equate it with outward things: possessions, experiences, achievements, and relationships. But here's what eludes them: blessedness isn't found in changing conditions and circumstances, but in an unchanging God.

And that's the message of Psalm 128. Here, we see three essential elements of true blessedness: its object, its fruit, and its source.

## The Object of Blessedness (v. 1)

"Blessed is everyone who fears the LORD, who walks in his ways!"

The fear of God is a central biblical motif. "Of all things that are to be known," writes Matthew Henry, "this is most evident, that God is to be feared, to be reverenced, served, and worshipped. This is so [much] the beginning of knowledge that those know nothing who do not know this."[3] But what exactly does it mean to fear God?

Years ago, my wife and I had the opportunity to visit Victoria Falls in Zimbabwe. On the spur of the moment, we decided to go kayaking, and our guide organized a breakfast for us on the banks of the beautiful Zambezi River. He then provided a brief training session, followed by a stern warning: "This is a wild river. You'll have no problem with the crocodiles, as long as you remain in your kayak. But the hippos are another matter entirely. If they feel threatened by you, they'll strike from below!" He proceeded to snap a twig, and announced (with what I think was a twinkle in his eye): "A hippo will vaporize your kayak!" I was ready to back out, but the peer pressure was too great, and so, we proceeded on our kayaking adventure.

It was delightful, until near the end of the trip when we entered a narrow stretch of the river. Suddenly, four sets of eyes appeared on the surface of the water. According to John Flavel, what I experienced at that moment is known as *natural* fear: "The trouble or perturbation of mind, from the comprehension of approaching evil or impending danger."[4] As we saw in the previous chapter, this kind of fear is an essential part of human nature—we fear what threatens us and, in response, we avoid what we fear.

But is this what it means to fear God? Are we supposed to view him as a danger to be avoided? To work through this, it's crucial to note that Scripture speaks of fearing God in two very different ways. This distinction is evident, for example, in Exodus 20. The Israelites are gathered at Mount Sinai, where they could see the fire and smoke, and hear the thunder. As a result, they're afraid. But Moses says to them, "Do not *fear*, for God has come to test you, that the *fear* of him may be before you, that you may sin not" (v. 20, italics mine). In short, Moses commands the people not to fear God, yet to fear God. How do we explain this apparent contradiction? "Mark it," says John Bunyan, "here are two fears: a fear forbidden and a fear commended."[5]

To put it another way, there's a wrong way and a right way to fear God: *ungodly* fear and *godly* fear. Ungodly fear flows from God wrongly perceived, whereas godly fear flows from God rightly perceived. Ungodly fear compels us to run from God, whereas godly fear compels us to run to God. Ungodly fear is based on a legal relationship we want to escape, whereas godly fear is based on a family relationship we want to cultivate. Making sense?

To get right to the point, ungodly fear flows from hate. When we think something threatens us, we hate it, and we seek to avoid or destroy it. Sadly, that's how many people fear God. They regard him as hazardous to their well-being. This kind of fear doesn't make any lasting impression upon the soul but causes people to amend their lives while secretly wishing God would go away. In marked contrast, godly fear flows from love. It doesn't arise from a perception of God as hazardous, but glorious. When the soul feels "a sweet taste of God's goodness," William Gouge says, and finds "that in his favor only all happiness consists, it is stricken with such an inward awe and reverence."[6]

We realize we've placed ourselves where God deserves to be—on the throne. We realize God has placed himself where we deserve to be—on the cross. By sovereign grace, he has made us one with his beloved Son. As a result, we enjoy the benefits of the cross. His forgiveness supersedes our sinfulness, and his righteousness supersedes our filthiness. From a deep sense of awe and reverence, we fear him. We seek to do what pleases him and avoid what displeases him. In other words, we seek to "walk in his ways." That's what it means to fear God.

## The Fruit of Blessedness (vv. 2–4)

According to the psalmist, the fruit of fearing God and walking in his ways is twofold.

## Fruitful Labor (v. 2)

"You shall eat the fruit of the labor of your hands; you shall be blessed, and it shall be well with you."

God designed labor for our good, but it now bears the effects of the fall (Genesis 2–3). For many people, it has become a tiring, draining, unrewarding, and unsatisfying pursuit. Bosses are unreasonable, employees are irresponsible, deadlines are impossible, meetings are postponed, messages are lost, tasks are mundane, expectations are too high, conditions are oppressive, spreadsheets don't balance, contractors exaggerate, and coworkers stab in the back. "What has a man from all the toil and striving of heart with which he toils under the sun? For all his days are full of sorrow, and his work is a vexation. Even in the night his heart does not rest" (Ecclesiastes 2:22–23).

But the curse is reversed for those who fear God. We "eat the fruit of the labor of [our] hands." This doesn't mean our work is suddenly free of all problems and struggles, but that God blesses our work to us. How? He provides for our needs; moreover, he gives us a measure of satisfaction in our labor. And so, we work hard at whatever God has called us to do. We do so to meet our needs, provide for our families, share with those in need, and—most importantly—serve God (1 Thessalonians 4:12; 1 Timothy 5:8; Ephesians 4:28; 6:7). In this way, our labor becomes a sacred calling—infused with dignity, purpose, and reward.

## Fruitful Home (v. 3)

"Your wife will be like a fruitful vine within your house; your children will be like olive shoots around your table."

The family is the basic unit of society, designed for our good (Genesis 2:18–25). As a consequence of the fall, however, it too suffers the negative effects of the curse (Gen. 3:16). Every home is dysfunctional to some degree, because every individual is sinful. Every home is fraught with challenges: unrealistic expectations, abrasive personalities, selfish attitudes, harsh words, long days, sleepless nights, dirty diapers, feuding siblings, and on it goes.

But the curse is reversed for those who fear God. When we live in the fear of God, the relationship between husband and wife is transformed. It's liberated from its modern-day caricature as a trap, chore, or burden. It's elevated into the realm of the divine. It's set apart as one of the most sacred callings the world has ever known. We see marriage for what it is: an illustration of the relationship between Christ and the church (Ephesians 5:22–33). God has embedded the gospel in the created order by embedding it in marriage. When we see a husband giving himself for his wife, we see Christ giving himself for his church.

The fear of God also transforms the relationship between parent and child. Parenthood becomes a calling, not a chore—a blessing, not an inconvenience. That is not to say that our homes are free of all problems. At times, we assume that if we read the right books, attend the right seminars, and adopt the right systems, then God will automatically bless our families. This assumption is a subtle form of legalism, whereby we assume our performance determines God's favor. But that isn't what the psalmist is saying. His point is that the fear of God transforms families. It humbles the proud, breaks the stubborn, and heals the wounded. It engenders meekness and compels forgiveness. Such a transformed family is a fruitful family.

## A Promise (v. 4)

"Behold, thus shall the man be blessed who fears the LORD."

I've driven in some crazy places. The city of Luanda, Angola, was one of the craziest. Why? No one paid any attention to the traffic laws. There was no speed limit. Stoplights didn't work most of the time, and when they did, red lights were ignored. Driving on the right side of the road was optional. During the morning rush hour, a multitude of cars converged at the various intersections throughout the city. It was sheer mayhem.

That's what life is like without the fear of God. A failure to walk in God's ways always results in mayhem on a *personal* and *societal* level.[7] People quickly lose all sense of the sacred. This loss is felt in every sphere, particularly in the home, as it weakens the institution of marriage. The result is an accelerated divorce rate, a rise in casual cohabitation, and a rise in alternative relationships. This weakening of the family unit results in public contempt for authority, which leads to a sharp rise in juvenile delinquency and a steady decline in a man's natural motivation to provide, protect, and procreate. In other words, manhood is emasculated. This kind of society becomes absorbed with the inordinate pursuit of pleasure—sexual and otherwise—and is marked by growing apathy for civic duty and responsibility and a decline in economic productivity and academic creativity. All of this leads to an unmanageable increase in public spending, because the government must compensate for the social sluggishness. It leads to a huge increase in military expenditures to fight real or imaginary foreign enemies, while the greatest enemy (moral decadence) goes unchecked and unchallenged at home. Does any of that sound familiar?

When we fear God, we "walk in his ways," meaning we conform ourselves to his will. We think, feel, value, desire, dream, plan, and live biblically. The result of harmonizing our lives with God's will is wisdom. "The fear of the LORD is the beginning of wisdom" (Proverbs 9:10). God's commandments are reflected in the world's order and structure; therefore, when we obey him, we harmonize our life with reality, resulting in true blessedness.

### The Source of Blessedness (vv. 5–6)

"The LORD bless you from Zion! May you see the prosperity of Jerusalem all the days of your life! May you see your children's children! Peace be upon Israel!"

Having described the fruit of blessedness in verses 2–4, the psalmist prays for it in verses 5–6. He prays for fruitful labor ("May you see the prosperity of Jerusalem all the days of your life!") and fruitful homes ("May you see your children's children!"). The psalmist makes it clear that God alone is the source of this blessedness: "The LORD bless you from Zion!" For ancient Israel, Zion is Jerusalem, where the temple stands in all its glory. For us, Zion is Christ and his church. *See Travel Tip #2.* The church is where the fear of God is birthed and nurtured and where the ways of God are proclaimed and expounded.

As a child, I was a huge fan of the Lone Ranger. I would rush home from school to watch old reruns on TV. The white hat, black mask, blue body suit, silver bullets—every boy's dream. The most compelling thing about the Lone Ranger was his strident independence. He didn't need anyone. By himself, he took on renegades, bandits, murderers, rustlers, and anyone else who dared to cross the line. Some of us think of ourselves as Lone Rangers, but there's no such thing in the body of Christ. The Christian journey isn't one of independence but dependence. That's the way God has designed it (Ephesians 4:11–16).

It's in the church, therefore, that we find the source of blessedness because in the church we come under the preaching of the Word— the means by which the Holy Spirit creates faith in the heart (John 3:3–5; Romans 9:16; 10:17). It's the appointed means by which God works in his people. "This, therefore, teaches us how to judge who fears the Lord," says John Bunyan. "They are those who learn, and who stand in awe of the Word. Those fear God who have, by the holy Word of God, the very form of that Word engraved upon the face of their souls."[8]

## Conclusion

We're made for eternity. We're made for something greater than ourselves—something greater than anything this world has to offer. Inherently, we know it's true. We long for something this world can't satisfy. Most people don't understand this. They're looking to the material and temporal to satisfy the spiritual and eternal. But God alone can provide true blessedness. This is what Christ has purchased for us: "For Christ also suffered once for sins, the righteous for the unrighteous, that he might bring us to God . . ." (1 Peter 3:18). God is ours.[9]

His power is ours to protect us. His wisdom is ours to direct us. His mercy is ours to pity us. His grace is ours to pardon us. His love is ours to refresh us. His joy is ours to satisfy us. His justice is ours to accept us as righteous in Christ. His faithfulness is ours to fulfill his promises to us. His majesty is ours to make us glorious forever. On top of all this, he's "our God forever and ever" (Psalm 48:14). He isn't our God for a day, week, month, or year, but "forever and ever." He isn't our God for a thousand years, but "forever and ever." He isn't our God for a million years, but "forever and ever." "Blessed are the people whose God is the LORD" (Psalm 144:15).

## Questions

1. Why do most people never find true blessedness?

2. What do you think would make you truly happy, content, and satisfied? Related to this, what do you dream about?

3. What is the difference between godly fear and ungodly fear? Do you see evidence of these two in your own life?

4. Is fear of God incompatible with love for God?

5. How should the fear of God sanctify your labor? Give examples.

6. How should the fear of God sanctify your home? Give examples.

7. What is the relationship between the fear of God and the Word of God?

8. Why is the fear of God the beginning of wisdom (Prov. 9:10)?

9. How can you turn this psalm into a prayer? List specific requests.

# 10

# Overcoming Abuse

## *Psalm 129*

[1] "Greatly have they afflicted me from my youth"—let Israel now say—
[2] "Greatly have they afflicted me from my youth, yet they have not prevailed against me.
[3] The plowers plowed upon my back; they made long their furrows."
[4] The LORD is righteous; he has cut the cords of the wicked.
[5] May all who hate Zion be put to shame and turned backward!
[6] Let them be like the grass on the housetops, which withers before it grows up,
[7] with which the reaper does not fill his hand nor the binder of sheaves his arms,
[8] nor do those who pass by say, "The blessing of the LORD be upon you! We bless you in the name of the LORD!"

Psalm 129 poses a problem for some people—perhaps even you. Why? It's numbered among the *imprecatory* psalms. That isn't a word we use every day. Here's a simple definition: to imprecate means to utter a curse. The imprecatory psalms, therefore, are those in which the author calls on God to curse his enemies. "Let death steal over them" (Psalm 55:15). "Break the teeth in their mouths" (Psalm 58:6). "Let them be blotted out of the book of the living" (Psalm 69:28). "May his children be fatherless and his wife a widow" (Psalm 109:9). Not very pleasant stuff! Why do some people struggle with this? Here's how I see it: they don't possess the necessary mental framework for understanding these psalms.

When my oldest daughter was three years old, she had a blue and red plastic ball. (If you're a parent, you know the one I'm talking about.) There were openings (in various shapes) on the ball, and it came with an assortment of yellow pieces (in varying shapes). The idea is to match the yellow pieces with the openings on the ball. It's riveting to watch a toddler attempt to shove a triangle in an opening the shape of a square. It doesn't matter how hard or how often she tries, it's never going to fit. Why? It's mismatched.

Unfortunately, that's often the way it is with our thinking. There's a mismatch between reality and our *perception* of reality. And that's why the imprecatory psalms are a problem for some. And so, I want to take the time to highlight five errors in thinking that make it extremely difficult to grasp these psalms—to make the pieces fit.

The first is a disjointed view of Scripture. Because of their failure to appreciate the harmony and continuity of Scripture, some people simply ignore the imprecatory psalms (and, for that matter, any other Old Testament passage they don't like). But we can't do that, for the simple reason that the New Testament accepts the Old Testament as fact. For example, Luke writes, "After destroying seven nations in the land of Canaan, [God] gave them their land as an inheritance" (Acts 13:19–20). There's no way around this: the New Testament accepts the annihilation of the Canaanites as historical fact, and—more to the point—as an act of God. The New Testament affirms the historicity and reliability of the Old Testament. More to the point, the New Testament actually quotes the imprecatory psalms (see Psalm 69 in John 2:17, 15:25, and Romans 11:9–10).

The second error is a distorted view of God. There are plenty of theological Marcionites out there. For those who don't know, Marcion lived a long time ago—the second century. In brief, he believed there were two gods—the god of the Old Testament (vengeful) and the god of the New Testament (merciful). The nice god came to deliver us from the not-so-nice god. Now, I've never met anyone who would express it in those terms, but that's more or less what many people believe. Either they deny the essential unity of the Father and the Son by believing that the Father is in view in the Old Testament whereas the Son is in view in the New Testament, or they collapse the numerical distinction between the Father and the Son by believing in a god who underwent a major personality change between the testaments. Either way, they deny (wittingly or not) the doctrine of the Trinity.

The third error is a deficient view of sin. In our day, social Darwinism has produced two major schools of thought to explain human behavior. The first is the *nurture* argument: we behave as we do because of our social environment. The second is the *nature* argument: we behave as we do because of our genetic makeup. Both schools of thought ultimately absolve the individual of any responsibility. This innocuous view of sin has infiltrated large segments of the church, thereby making God's judgment seem preposterous. But the Bible paints a very different portrait of our condition. It makes it clear that our problem resides within. Nurture and nature might exacerbate the problem, but they aren't the problem. This issue is our depraved heart. In every sin, there's a spirit of atheism, rebellion, hatred, and murder. Until we grasp this, the *imprecatory* psalms remain a closed book.

The fourth error is a diminished view of justice. Our society's concept of justice has undergone a dramatic shift in the past few decades. Today, most people identify the chief purpose of justice as rehabilitation, not retribution. Because of this shift in thinking, the concept of God's wrath is now incompatible with people's *sensibilities*. It's true that we must differentiate between personal vengeance and moral repugnance, petty vindictiveness and perfect righteousness, self-seeking revenge and God-glorifying justice. At the same time, however, we must not fail to see God's justice as the expression of his goodness in his condemnation of sinners. The imprecatory psalms provide a preview of what will happen at the final judgment. Christ will come from heaven with his mighty angels in flaming fire, "inflicting vengeance on those who do not know God and on those who do not obey the gospel" (2 Thessalonians 1:8).

The fifth error is a defective definition of forgiveness. A concept known as "therapeutic forgiveness" came into vogue in the 1980s.[1] Simply put, it defines forgiveness as ceasing to feel anger or resentment toward a person who has wronged you. This might seem harmless enough, but it isn't. Why not? It has turned forgiveness into an emotion. This definition is now accepted orthodoxy within the church, meaning many professing Christians perceive God's forgiveness as an emotional change. How does this play out? Well, God is forgiving, meaning he isn't angry with me. He forgives me unconditionally. Sound familiar? But this concept of forgiveness is completely foreign to Scripture. Biblical forgiveness isn't an emotion, but a transaction. How does God forgive? There are two essential ingredients: justice and repentance. God forgives those who repent on the basis of his satisfied justice in Christ's substitutionary sacrifice. *See Travel Tip #1.* As a result, they're reconciled and restored to him. But there's no restoration without forgiveness, and there's no forgiveness without repentance. All that to say this: God's forgiveness is *conditional*, not unconditional. Until this is understood, the imprecatory psalms remain a mental roadblock.

I pray all the yellow pieces are now inside the red and blue ball. If so, we're ready for the actual content of Psalm 129. We're going to follow three stages in the psalmist's thought-flow.

### The Psalmist's Affliction (vv. 1–3)

"'Greatly have they afflicted me from my youth'—let Israel now say—'Greatly have they afflicted me from my youth, yet they have not prevailed against me. The plowers plowed upon my back; they made long their furrows.'"

Here, the psalmist mentions five details concerning affliction. It's *corporate*: "let Israel now say." In other words, the psalmist expresses the experience of the nation as a whole. It's *severe*: "greatly." The psalmist uses this term twice so he isn't speaking of some trivial inconvenience. This is a life-altering, heart-wrenching, mind-tormenting, pain-inducing, anguish-inflicting ordeal. It's *persistent*: "since my youth." When was Israel young? It's likely a reference to Egypt. The psalmist, therefore, is reminding the people of their forefathers' bondage. Their national history is a story of suffering. It's *personal*: "they." The psalmist isn't talking about some natural disaster or calamity, nor is he talking about some unfortunate set of circumstances.

These people have been intentionally victimized. It's *brutal*: "they plowed upon my back." Conquering armies would inflict this kind of torture upon defeated enemies. And so, it's possible the psalmist uses this imagery to magnify the horror of their affliction. It's also possible he uses it by way of a metaphor for whipping. Either way, the affliction is brutal—ruthless.

What does he say in the midst of it all? "Yet they have not prevailed against me." Why? That brings us to the second stage in his thought-flow.

### The Psalmist's Expectation (v. 4)

"The LORD is righteous; he has cut the cords of the wicked."

What does the psalmist mean? When he claims that God is righteous, he's saying that God is wonderfully faithful. In what sense? What has God done? He has remembered his people. How? "He has cut the cords of the wicked." These cords likely refer to what the psalmist mentioned in the previous verse—the cords that attach the plow to the oxen. God has severed these cords. In other words, God has delivered his people from their oppressors. And so, God's righteousness is seen in his preservation of his people. But it's also seen in his punishment of his enemies. And that brings us to the third stage in the psalmist's thought-flow.

### The Psalmist's Imprecation (vv. 5–8)

"May all who hate Zion be put to shame and turned backward! Let them be like the grass on the housetops, which withers before it grows up, with which the reaper does not fill his hand nor the binder of sheaves his arms, nor do those who pass by say, 'The blessing of the LORD be upon you! We bless you in the name of the LORD!'"

The psalmist asks God to put Israel's tormentors to shame. He uses a word picture to explain what he has in mind: he wants "them to be like the grass on the housetops." The grass is gathered, thatched, and placed on the rooftop. With a little rain and sunshine, it actually continues to grow—but not for long. Detached from the soil, it soon withers, browns, and rots. When it does, it's no longer of any use and so is quickly replaced.

Do you understand the psalmist's word picture? He wants his enemies to be like this grass. They might prosper (be lifted up) for a short time, but ultimately they'll wither like useless grass. They will never "know the blessing of the LORD." This is the psalmist's prayer.

## Conclusion

Stepping back, we discover that this psalm is ultimately fulfilled in Christ and his church. *See Travel Tip #2.* Like the psalmist, Christ experiences terrible affliction: "I gave my back to those who strike, and my cheeks to those who pull out the beard; I hid not my face from disgrace and spitting" (Isaiah 50:6). Like the psalmist, Christ looks to God: "But the Lord GOD helps me; therefore I have not been disgraced; therefore I have set my face like a flint, and I know that I shall not be put to shame" (Isaiah 50:7). Like the psalmist, Christ entrusts his enemies to God's judgment: "Behold, all of them will wear out like a garment; the moth will eat them up" (Isaiah 50:9).

How do we react to those who victimize us? What do we say to those who are the victims of crime, abandonment, slander, betrayal, or abuse? Here's the starting point: we remain focused on the cross—Christ's plowed back. When we do, the result is fourfold.

First, Christ's plowed back enables us to escape the prison of the past. How? Christ now shapes our identity. We're one with him in his death, burial, and resurrection. Because we're one with him, we're justified in God's sight and adopted into God's family. That makes us God's *beloved*. We no longer define ourselves by how others have mistreated us in the past. What a tremendous encouragement to those who have been the victims of unspeakable abuse. These experiences don't determine your worth or define your identity. You're one with Christ. You define yourself by what God says about you in Christ.

Second, Christ's plowed back moves us to squash hatred and bitterness. It enables us to mortify—or destroy—the desire for personal revenge. We don't repay evil for evil (Romans 12:17). An unwillingness to destroy the desire for revenge breaks down the door to the heart, leaving it wide open for other sins to enter. An unwillingness to mortify the desire for revenge reveals deep-rooted pride and prevents spiritual growth and maturity. An unwillingness to smother the desire for revenge belittles God's grace as displayed in the gospel. At the foot of the cross, we're humbled. In the shadow of the cross, Christ engenders meekness, enabling us to seek the good of others.

Third, Christ's plowed back compels us to offer *conditional* forgiveness. When we contemplate the cross, we're crushed to the ground. We're overwhelmed by God's love for us. And we're compelled to extend compassion to others—even those who have hated and abused us: "Forgiving one another, as God in Christ forgave you" (Ephesians 4:32). How does God forgive us? Where there's repentance, there's forgiveness. Where there's forgiveness, there's restoration. That's a transaction. We offer this same conditional forgiveness to those who've wronged us. If they repent, we forgive them. And what if they refuse to repent? Well, that brings us to the next point.

Fourth, Christ's plowed back strengthens us to wait for the Avenger. "Beloved, never avenge yourselves, but leave it to the wrath of God, for it is written, 'Vengeance is mine, I will repay, says the Lord'" (Romans 12:19). Although it might seem that those who abuse and misuse others are escaping the consequences of their actions, Paul assures us that God is a glorious Avenger. In the case of those who refuse to repent, there's no forgiveness—only the certain expectation of judgment.

This was Paul's own outlook. On one occasion, he writes, "Alexander the coppersmith did me great harm; the Lord will repay him according to his deeds" (2 Timothy 4:14). How did Alexander harm Paul? Slander? Imprisonment? Torture? We don't know the details, but we do know it involved "great harm." Now, please take note: Paul doesn't forgive Alexander. He doesn't offer him *unconditional* forgiveness. Undoubtedly, Paul mortified his desire for personal revenge and would have been kind to Alexander if given the opportunity. Undoubtedly, Paul would have forgiven Alexander if he had repented of his sin. But without repentance, true biblical forgiveness is impossible. And so, what comforts Paul in the face of Alexander's obstinate sin? Paul rests in the undeniable fact that God "will repay him according to his deeds."

"The terrible Avenger is to be praised," says C. H. Spurgeon, "as well as the loving Redeemer. Against this the sympathy of man's evil heart with sin rebels; it cries out for an effeminate God in whom pity has strangled justice. But the well-instructed servants of Jehovah praise him in all the aspects of his character, whether terrible or tender."[2]

## Questions

1. Are you the victim of abuse?

2. Do you struggle with rage, despair, or bitterness? If so, why?

3. What is biblical forgiveness? Explain the essential elements.

4. Why do so many people struggle to understand the nature of God's justice?

5. Is there such a thing as vengeance?

6. How does the psalmist find peace, even when he's victimized?

7. How do we see this same attitude portrayed in Christ?

8. How does looking to Christ help us in dealing with anger?

9. How does looking to Christ help us "escape the prison cell of the past"?

10. How can you turn this psalm into a prayer? List specific requests.

# 11

# Confessing Sin

## *Psalm 130*

¹ Out of the depths I cry to you, O LORD!
² O Lord, hear my voice! Let your ears be attentive to the voice of my pleas for mercy!
³ If you, O LORD, should mark iniquities, O Lord, who could stand?
⁴ But with you there is forgiveness, that you may be feared.
⁵ I wait for the LORD, my soul waits, and in his word I hope;
⁶ my soul waits for the Lord more than watchmen for the morning, more than watchmen for the morning.
⁷ O Israel, hope in the LORD!
For with the LORD there is steadfast love, and with him is plentiful redemption.
⁸ And he will redeem Israel from all his iniquities.

According to what I've read, Psalm 130 was the favorite psalm of Augustine, Martin Luther, and John Calvin. I realize not everyone gets excited when they hear those three names, but I feel it's extremely significant that these lofty theologians had such a high regard for this psalm. One of the greatest theologians in the history of the English-speaking world, John Owen, published a 320-page book on this psalm in the year 1668. It was precious to him because God used it powerfully at a specific juncture in his life. Owen recalls:

I preached Christ for some years, when I had very little (if any) experimental acquaintance with access to God through Christ. But the Lord was pleased to visit me with sore affliction, whereby I was brought to the mouth of the grave, and under which my soul was oppressed with horror and darkness. But God graciously relieved my spirit by a powerful application of Psalm 130:4, "But with you there is forgiveness that you may be feared."[1]

I trust Owen's personal testimony has created some sense of anticipation on your part, but we need to begin by making a couple of introductory remarks regarding the psalmist's subject and style. The subject of Psalm 130 is repentance, a subject that, sadly, has fallen on hard times. Far too many people are in the grip of what's known as the feel-good doctrine of automatic forgiveness. Simply put, they believe in a gospel that promises forgiveness without requiring change. They're sorely mistaken. We must never confuse repentance with regret—being sorry *mentally*. Likewise, we must never confuse repentance with remorse—being sorry *mentally* and *emotionally*. Repentance is being sorry *mentally*, *emotionally*, and *volitionally*. In other words, repentance involves change. We must not err here. We've only repented of our sin when we're prepared to let go of our sin.

Next, we consider the psalmist's style, which is extreme—in a good sense of the word. He leads us from the depths of despair to the heights of elation; from sorrow to jubilation; tribulation to devotion. He leads us from the crushing depths of man's depravity to the soaring heights of God's mercy. How does he accomplish all that? It begins with a cry.

### The Psalmist's Cry to God (vv. 1–2)

"Out of the depths I cry to you, O LORD! O Lord, hear my voice! Let your ears be attentive to the voice of my pleas for mercy!"

Here, the psalmist cries to God. Why? How? What? That's what we want to know.

### Why He Cries (v. 1)

"Out of the depths I cry to you, O LORD."

What are the "depths"? We find similar language in Psalm 88:6–7, "You have put me in the depths of the pit, in the regions dark and deep. Your wrath lies heavy upon me, and you overwhelm me with all your waves." I believe it's the same idea in our verse—that is, the "depths" speak of the waves of God's displeasure toward the psalmist's sin. As these waves encompass him, he feels as though he's drowning, he's struggling with a disturbed conscience, tormented mind, and troubled heart.

Now, this graphic description of spiritual turmoil poses a problem for some Christians. Does God really put his people in the depths of the pit and overwhelm them with the waves of his displeasure? For many, these things are unimaginable. They're adamant that God never treats his people like this. I disagree. I admit this is a *tricky truth*, so let me ease into it slowly by asking a few questions. Does God love you? Does God love you even when you sin? Is God ever angry or displeased with you? Do you have your answers? Good. A while back, I sat with a man—a professing Christian, and an acknowledged adulterer. I told him God was displeased with him—even angry with him. The man was shocked—offended. He proceeded to quote from Romans 8:39, "Nothing can separate us from the love of God in Christ Jesus our Lord," and insisted that God loved him, and was never displeased with him. Is that true? Possibly. It depends on what we mean by *love*. Here's the *tricky truth*: God loves his people in two ways.

First, God loves his people *unconditionally*. This is God's delight in his people as we stand in Christ. This love doesn't change. It can't increase or decrease. And that's what Paul has in mind in Romans 8:39. A story has been told about Charles Spurgeon walking through the English countryside with a friend. As they strolled along, the famous evangelist noticed a barn with a weather vane on its roof. At the top of the vane were these words: "God is love." Spurgeon told his companion he thought this was a rather inappropriate place for such a message. "Weather vanes are changeable, but God's love is constant," he said. "I don't agree with you about those words, Charles," replied his friend. "You misunderstood the meaning. That sign is indicating a wonderful truth: Regardless of which way the wind blows, God is love."

Second, God loves his people *conditionally*. God delights in the holiness that grows in his people from the seed of his grace. This love does change. It can increase or decrease. Christ declares, "Whoever has my commandments and keeps them, he it is who loves me. And he who loves me will be loved by my Father, and I will love him and manifest myself to him" (John 14:21). Again, he declares, "If you keep my commandments, you will abide in my love" (John 15:10). Clearly, the love Christ describes here is conditional upon obedience.

And so, God loves his people in two ways. Are you still with me? When we disobey God, what happens? On the one hand, God's love for us doesn't change. That's his *unconditional* love—his delight in us in Christ. On the other hand, his love for us does change. That's his *conditional* love—his delight in the holiness in us. For the Christian, there is what John Owen calls "an abiding, dwelling sense of God's love upon the heart."[2] But it's conditional, meaning we can lose it on account of our sin. When we do, the result is trouble, anxiety, and restlessness. That's the psalmist's experience. He feels as though he's drowning in the waves of God's displeasure. As a result, he cries from the depths.

Have you ever experienced anything like this? Restless nights, frayed nerves, mood swings? What about a long face, a lack of joy and peace, disinterest in prayer and study, avoidance of deeper things, or an unwillingness to get close to others for fear of discovery? Have you ever found yourself withdrawing from Christian fellowship or dismissing godliness as legalism and extremism? What about harshness in censuring others? Do you know what these things are? They're marks of a troubled conscience, arising from a refusal to deal with past sins, to mortify present lusts, to release future worries, or to obey what God commands. Your sin has dampened your enjoyment of that "dwelling sense of God's love upon the heart." Straight to the point, you're in the depths!

## How He Cries (v. 2)

"O Lord, hear my voice."

The psalmist is pleading with God to "hear" him, and he doesn't attempt to minimize or trivialize the severity of his sin. He doesn't manifest even a hint of presumption or entitlement. What a crucial example for those of us who attempt to excuse our sin. Some of us do so by convincing ourselves that our sin is shaped by circumstances: "I'm a victim of circumstances beyond my control! If things were different, I wouldn't do what I do." Really? Here's a news flash: circumstances don't make us do what we do, but they can show us what we already are. "Water in the glass looks clear," says Thomas Watson, "but set it on the fire, and the scum soon boils up."[3]

Some of us excuse our sin by claiming there is safety in numbers: "Everyone does it. I'm just like everyone else. So, what have I got to worry about?" That kind of thinking is riddled with problems. A cancer patient doesn't derive any comfort from the fact that lots of people have cancer. If we comfort ourselves by looking at the widespread prevalence of our sin in others, we're deceiving ourselves.

Some of us excuse our sin by convincing ourselves that it's comparatively minimal: "I've never done what that person has done. My offenses are tame in comparison to his." When we fall into that way of thinking, we've merely added self-righteousness to our long list of sins. We've become like the Pharisee: "O God, I thank you that I am not like other men" (Luke 18:11).

Some of us excuse our sin by convincing ourselves that it's totally normal: "To err is human. So what can anyone expect?" That reflects a serious misunderstanding of the nature of sin. God made Adam and Eve perfect, meaning their human nature was perfect. Fallen human nature is the result (you guessed it) of the fall. Sin, therefore, isn't a testimony to our humanity but our depravity. That is to say, there's nothing *normal* about sin.

The psalmist has moved well beyond these kinds of excuses for his sin. He knows he has offended God, and he knows what he deserves. He doesn't bargain or negotiate. He doesn't minimize or trivialize. He doesn't attempt to excuse himself or justify himself. He knows the sentence of *guilty* hangs over him. The weight is too heavy to bear. And so, he pleads with God to hear his voice.

**What He Cries (v. 2)**

"Let your ears be attentive to the voice of my pleas for mercy."

Here, we discover the content of the psalmist's cry: he wants mercy. God's grace is his goodness bestowed *apart from* merit, but his mercy is his goodness bestowed *contrary to* merit. As sinners, the only thing we deserve from God is punishment. Every taste of his goodness, therefore, is an expression of his mercy. The psalmist wants God to deal with him on the basis of mercy—contrary to what he deserves.

Because of our sin, this is the only appeal we can make to God. When the Pharisee and the tax collector visit the temple to pray, they approach God from two very different angles (Luke 18:10–13). The Pharisee seeks to stand before God on the basis of his own merit: "God, I thank you that I am not like other men." But the tax collector asks God to deal with him contrary to merit: "God, be merciful to me, a sinner!" As John Bunyan rightly observes, the Pharisee and the tax collector are "two men in whose condition the whole world is comprehended."[4] In other words, there are only two kinds of people in the world: Pharisees—the proud who ignore their sin, and tax collectors—the humble who confess their sin. Which of the two returned to his house "justified"? The tax collector! "Everyone who exalts himself will be humbled," declares Christ, "but the one who humbles himself will be exalted."

**The Psalmist's Appeal to God (vv. 3–4)**

"If you, O LORD, should mark iniquities, O Lord, who could stand? But with you there is forgiveness, that you may be feared."

Under deep conviction for sin, the psalmist cries out to God for mercy. He's confident that God will respond to him. Why? He understands the nature of God's forgiveness.

**The Need for God's Forgiveness (v. 3)**

"If you, O LORD, should mark iniquities, O Lord, who could stand?"

In the first part of this clause, the psalmist addresses God as the "LORD" (*Yah*), thereby pointing to God's eternality and immortality.

His point is that God sees all. In the second part of the clause, the psalmist addresses God as the "Lord" (*Adonai*), thereby pointing to God's authority and sovereignty. His point is that God judges all. There is, therefore, what John Owen calls "a double marking of sin."[5] God sees and judges our iniquities.

The psalmist's point is obvious: if this God who sees all and judges all were to "mark" (i.e., reserve for punishment) our iniquities, we wouldn't be able to stand—judicially speaking—in his presence for even a moment. To put it another way, if God were to deal with us on the basis of what we truly deserve, his holiness would consume us. This harsh reality serves to highlight the psalmist's next statement. I remember looking at engagement rings about a quarter-century ago. As I entered the jewelry store in our local mall, I noticed that all of the rings were displayed on a black velvet backdrop. Why? The blackness set off the diamonds' beauty and brilliance. That's what we have in this statement. The psalmist uses the darkness of our iniquity and certainty of God's judgment to magnify the beauty of God's forgiveness.

### The Certainty of God's Forgiveness (v. 4)

"But with you there is forgiveness . . ."

Essentially, the psalmist's point is that forgiveness is God's nature. "The LORD, the LORD, a God merciful and gracious, slow to anger, and abounding in steadfast love and faithfulness, keeping steadfast love for thousands, forgiving iniquity and transgression and sin" (Exodus 34:6–7). Because forgiveness is God's nature, God is forgiving. We don't need to coax or convince him to forgive. The psalmist, therefore, is confident that as he cries from the depths for mercy God will hear him.

### The Fruit of God's Forgiveness (v. 4)

"That you may be feared . . ."

We considered what it means to fear God in conjunction with Psalm 128 and noted that godly fear arises from an experience of God's goodness. We realize we've placed ourselves where God deserves to be—on the throne and that God has placed himself where we deserve to be—on the cross. By sovereign grace, he has made us one with his beloved Son. As a result, we enjoy the benefits of the cross as his forgiveness supersedes our sinfulness, and his righteousness supersedes our filthiness. From a deep sense of awe and reverence, we fear him. We seek to do what pleases him and avoid what displeases him. In other words, we seek to *walk in his ways*. All that to say, God's forgiveness is transformative. It causes us to fear him. We fear to lose one look of his love, one word of his kindness, one touch of his tenderness. "Great love," says John Owen, "springs out of great forgiveness."[6]

This transformative effect of forgiveness is crucial. Why? Lots of people *lament* their sin. They lament their poor choices and the mess they've made of their lives. They lament the negative consequences of their sins—the suffering, disappointment, frustration, and shame. When we lament, we feel the pain, anguish, and discomfort and just want the mess to go away. We're frustrated and perplexed and wish things were different. But we dare not confuse lamenting with repenting. Esau lamented. Saul lamented. Ahab lamented. Judas lamented. But none of them ever repented.

We repent when we see our sin without making excuses. When Adam and Eve saw their sin in the Garden, they made lots of excuses (Genesis 3:9–13). Adam blamed Eve, and Eve blamed the serpent. Their descendants have emulated their example ever since, inventing a myriad of excuses for their sin. We're a bottomless pit of excuses. But, when the Holy Spirit works in our heart, the excuses stop. We see our sin as God sees it and understand that it springs from our heart's departure from God. Sin is rebellion against God's sovereignty, arrogance against God's power, unrighteousness against God's justice. It's ignorance against God's wisdom, stubbornness against God's will, evil against God's goodness, transgression against God's law. Sin is hatred against God's love and murder against God's being. When we see our sin as it truly is, we cry with David from the depths: "I have sinned against the LORD" (2 Sam. 12:13). Basking in the glory of God's forgiveness, we fear him by forsaking our sin. That's repentance.

## The Psalmist's Hope in God (vv. 5–6)

"I wait for the LORD, my soul waits, and in his word I hope; my soul waits for the Lord more than watchmen for the morning, more than watchmen for the morning."

Three times in these verses, the psalmist says he "waits" for God. Initially, that might seem confusing. He has cried to God for mercy, and he has appealed to God for forgiveness. Hasn't he received these things? Yes. So why's he waiting for God? We dare not miss this: as far as the psalmist is concerned, God's mercy and forgiveness are merely a means to end and that end is God. The absence of God from the psalmist's soul is what initially casts him into the depths. Now, he's anticipating the return of God's refreshing and comforting presence. He's waiting for the return of "an abiding, dwelling sense of God's love upon the heart." How does he wait?

For starters, he waits *confidently*: "I wait for the LORD, my soul waits, and in his word I hope." The psalmist's wait isn't baseless or pointless but has a sure object: God's Word. He knows God has promised to forgive those who repent. In addition, the psalmist waits *longingly*: "My soul waits for the Lord more than the watchman for the morning, more than watchman for the morning." Many years ago, I spent a summer working at Ontario Hydro in Toronto. I worked on a three-week rotating shift: 8:00 a.m. to 4:00 p.m., 4:00 p.m. to midnight, and midnight to 8 a.m. The first night of the third shift was a killer, because I would be up twenty-four hours straight. Some of you know what that's like. My eyes were heavy, my head fuzzy, and my body weary. I anxiously waited for the sunrise. That's the idea here. The psalmist knows God is coming, and so, he waits longingly, anxiously, expectantly. When God does return, the psalmist moves from the depths of despair to the heights of elation.

## The Psalmist's Invitation (vv. 7–8)

"O Israel, hope in the LORD! For with the LORD there is steadfast love, and with him is plentiful redemption. And he will redeem Israel from all his iniquities."

The psalmist's experience of God's mercy overflows into an invitation: "O Israel, hope in the LORD!" He gives two powerful incentives for doing so.

**Why God Forgives (v. 7)**

"For with the LORD there is steadfast love."

Do you remember the distinction between God's conditional and unconditional love? Here, we're focusing on the latter: God's unchanging and unwavering love for us in Christ. In order to appreciate God's steadfast love (*hesed*), we must differentiate between human love and divine love.[7] As humans, we need love just like we need food and water. We can't live without it. Therefore, when we love others, we expect them to love us in return, meaning our love is always self-serving to some degree. But God's love isn't like that. It's never self-serving. As Christians, we believe God is triune. We confess it in the Apostle's Creed and when we're baptized in the name of the Father and of the Son and of the Holy Spirit (Matthew 28:19). We believe the Father is God, the Son is God, and the Holy Spirit is God. We also believe the Father isn't the Son, the Son isn't the Holy Spirit, and the Holy Spirit isn't the Father. That is to say, we believe God is three distinct persons in one substance.

God's tri-unity is crucial for understanding his love. Why? It means God is the object of his love. The Father, the Son, and the Holy Spirit dwell in an eternity of mutual delight. That means God is satisfied in himself. And that means he doesn't need to love us, nor does he need us to love him. Simply put, he doesn't gain anything from loving us. That realization should comfort us, because that's the kind of love we need. We need someone to love us who doesn't actually need us. God has that kind of love in himself. And here's the wonderful thing: he lavishes it upon us. We don't need to earn or merit God's love. We don't need to worry that God's love for us will change. We don't need to worry that God's love for us is contingent upon our performance. Why? God's love for us in Christ is steadfast.

**How God Forgives (v. 8)**

"And with him there is plentiful redemption."

What does the psalmist know of redemption? He knows enough. The Feast of Passover, for example, clearly revealed the nature of redemption. Prior to the Exodus, God sent ten plagues upon the land of Egypt, ending with the death of the firstborn. To avoid that particular judgment, the Israelites had to celebrate the Passover by selecting an unblemished male from the sheep or goats, killing it, then painting its blood on their doorposts and lintels. Because of that blood, God spared the firstborn of the Israelites. It was not their works that saved them, but the actual sprinkling of blood. They were sinners, as were the Egyptians, and God in his justice might have punished them by taking away the life of their firstborn. He was pleased, however, to show mercy, accepting the life of the Passover lamb as a substitute.

The Passover became one of seven annual feasts celebrated by the Israelites. Coupled with an elaborate sacrificial system, these feasts provided a glimpse into the nature of redemption: "For the life of the flesh is in the blood, and I have given it for you on the altar to make atonement for your souls, for it is the blood that makes atonement by the life" (Leviticus 17:11). The entire system encouraged the believing Israelite to look forward in anticipation of God's promised deliverer.

With Christ's arrival, the shadow gave way to the substance (Colossians 2:17). *See Travel Tip #2.* Paul affirms that "Christ our Passover lamb" has been sacrificed (1 Corinthians 5:7). When Christ shed his blood, he paid the penalty for our sin, which God had reckoned to him. God's offended justice was fully satisfied by Christ's sacrifice under divine judgment righteously due to us. As we sing:

My sin – oh, the bliss of this glorious tho't:
My sin, not in part but the whole,
Is nailed to the cross, and I bear it no more,
Praise the Lord, praise the Lord, O my soul![8]

On this basis, God, "in his divine forbearance" passed over former sins (Romans 3:25). That means he passed over the sins of his people—Noah, Abraham, Sarah, Isaac, Jacob, Moses, Rahab, Ruth,

David, and others. He forgave them on the basis of what Christ was going to accomplish upon the cross. And now, God forgives us on the basis of what Christ has accomplished upon the cross. Forgiveness doesn't mean God acts like nothing happened, nor does it mean that he lessens the consequences of our sins. It means that he dissolves the obligation to punishment, on the basis of Christ's redeeming work.

## Conclusion

That's all the motivation we need to cry to God from the depths of a disturbed conscience, tormented mind, and troubled heart. When we sin, we're guilty of disobeying God's law, despising God's goodness, and grieving God's Spirit. Moreover, we're guilty of provoking the One who's the source of all life, light, joy, peace, and comfort. But we cry to God for mercy, knowing that he redeems us from all our iniquities.

Redemption is God's greatest work, far outshining his works of creation and providence. It's his masterpiece, revealing his manifold perfections, that gives him the greatest delight and greatest glory. Are you in the clutches of worry, lust, envy, anger, bitterness? Are you struggling with addiction? Are you chiefly concerned with your personal ease and comfort? Are you guilty of sexual indulgence? Are you characterized by destructive patterns in the way you think and live? Are you in the depths? "O Israel, hope in the LORD! For with the LORD there is steadfast love, and with him is plentiful redemption."

### Questions

1. What is the cause of the psalmist's cry? Can you relate?
2. God loves His people in two ways. Explain.
3. Do you ever excuse your sin? If so, how?
4. Why can we approach God confidently when humbled for our sin?
5. How does God's forgiveness affect you?
6. What is the difference between lamenting and repenting? Do you see the difference in your life?

7. What is the basis of forgiveness?

8. How does this psalm encourage you in the midst of your struggle with sin?

9. How can you turn this psalm into a prayer? List specific requests.

# 12

# Cultivating Hope

## *Psalm 131*

[1] O LORD, my heart is not lifted up; my eyes are not raised too high;
I do not occupy myself with things too great and too marvelous for me.
[2] But I have calmed and quieted my soul, like a weaned child with
its mother;
like a weaned child is my soul within me.
[3] O Israel, hope in the LORD from this time forth and forevermore.

Viktor Frankl, an Austrian neurologist and psychiatrist, wrote
of his years imprisoned in the horrors of Auschwitz and Dachau,
describing cold, fear, pain, vermin, starvation, and exhaustion, but
said he survived because he never lost hope. He also wrote of what
would happen when a prisoner did lose hope: he would refuse to get
out of bed, refuse to dress or wash, turning a deaf ear to his friends'
pleading and his captors' threatening. He would simply lie in his bed
until he died, having surrendered all hope.[1]

Hope is absolutely crucial to Christians. When it weakens, the
result is always the same: spiritual inertia. It's imperative, therefore, to remember that we're on a journey—still a long way from
home—and that hope is the fuel that keeps us going. We must guard
and nurture it. But what exactly is hope? Oftentimes, we're saddled
with clumsy definitions and so don't quite understand the concept
of hope. Is it to believe that anything can happen? Is it to expect that

things will get better? Is it to wish for something against all odds? Is it to maintain a sunny outlook despite what happens? No, it isn't any of those things. Simply put, to hope is to wait confidently and expectantly for what God has promised. *See Travel Tip #3.* I want you to notice a couple of things about this definition.

To begin with, it means that hope is fixed on God's promises: "Whatever was written in former days was written for our instruction, that through endurance and through the encouragement of the Scriptures we might have hope" (Romans 15:4). The Bible shows us what God has promised. He has promised eternal spiritual blessings—unconditionally (Ephesians 1:3). And he has promised present temporal blessings—conditionally (Matthew 6:33). These present-day blessings are provided based upon what he deems best for his eternal glory and our spiritual good.

Furthermore, the definition means that hope is fixed on God's attributes: "For God alone, O my soul, wait in silence, for my hope is from him" (Psalm 62:5). There's no hope if God isn't immutable; his promises might be altered. There's no hope if God isn't sovereign; his promises might be thwarted. There's no hope if God isn't omniscient; his promises might be misdirected. There's no hope if God isn't omnipotent; his promises might be hindered. But he is all of these things—and much more. "Who in the skies can be compared to the LORD? Who among the heavenly beings is like the LORD?" (Psalm 89:6). The mightiest of angels and the greatest of humans are but a shadow of a shadow in comparison to God and less than nothing in relation to him. God alone is infinite in power, wisdom, and goodness.

This kind of hope serves as a strong anchor to the soul: "We have this as a sure and steadfast anchor of the soul, a hope that enters into the inner place behind the curtain, where Jesus has gone as a forerunner on our behalf" (Hebrews 6:19–20a). What purpose does an anchor serve? It keeps the ship steady in turbulent waters. Similarly, hope provides stability when the circumstances of life threaten to overwhelm us.

That's why David declares in Psalm 131, "O Israel, hope in the LORD from this time forth and forevermore" (v. 3). He encourages

God's people to wait confidently and expectantly for what God has promised. How? We find the answer in the earlier part of the psalm. Basically, David affirms that we must come to terms with two things. First, we must come to terms with our pride by subduing and humbling our heart (v. 1). Second, we must come to terms with God's providence by calming and quieting our soul (v. 2). It's impossible to wait confidently and expectantly for what God has promised when our heart is inflated and our soul is troubled.

## Subduing and Humbling the Heart (v. 1)

"O LORD, my heart is not lifted up; my eyes are not raised too high; I do not occupy myself with things too great and too marvelous for me."

In this verse, David makes three claims—each revealing something about the nature of pride. David's claim that his "heart is not lifted up" reveals that pride is innate; it resides in the heart. David's claim that his "eyes are not raised too high" reveals that pride usually leads to ambition—craving for acceptance, admiration, and adulation. And David's claim that he does not concern himself "with things too great and too marvelous" reveals that pride usually leads to presumption—aspiring after "great" things and searching out "marvelous" things.

When it's all said and done, pride is the sin of all sins. Satan rebelled because he wanted to be like God. Adam and Eve did the same thing. Ever since, man has been in love with *self*. In their state of innocence in the garden, Adam and Eve were directed by a *true* self-love. They loved happiness. Because they viewed God as their greatest good—their greatest source of happiness—they loved God and, therefore, their affections were well-directed. Since the fall, however, our soul has been directed by a *false* self-love. We still love happiness. However, we no longer view God as the greatest good; instead we see ourselves in that role. Because we no longer love God, our affections are ill-directed.

This misplaced love lies at the root of every sin and opposes God by usurping his glory. That's why pride is the object of God's hatred (Proverbs 16:5). "God abhors other sinners," warns Thomas Manton, "but against the proud he professes open defiance and hostility."[2] Pride is our biggest problem—not poor health, rebellious children, difficult neighbors, broken relationships, financial problems, unfulfilled dreams, or daunting afflictions.

David knows it, and he knows his pride makes it impossible for him to "hope in the LORD" in the midst of affliction. And so, he claims to have subdued and humbled his heart. This isn't a claim to perfection, but an acknowledgment of his sincere pursuit of humility. According to Jonathan Edwards, humility is "a habit of mind and heart corresponding to our comparative unworthiness and vileness before God, or a sense of our own comparative meanness in his sight, with the disposition to a behavior answerable thereto."[3] Edwards mentions two kinds of humility: natural humility and moral humility.[4]

Edwards says natural humility arises from a perception of our "meanness" (or smallness) as creatures before God. In other words, it arises when we compare ourselves to God's *natural* excellence—his greatness. We're weak in comparison to his power, foolish in comparison to his wisdom, ignorant in comparison to his knowledge, small in comparison to his sovereignty. Second, Edwards speaks of moral humility, which arises from a perception of our "vileness" as sinners before God. In other words, it arises when we compare ourselves to God's *moral* excellence—his goodness. We recognize that we've sinned against God's grace and mercy and that we're without moral virtues adequate to commend ourselves to God. As a result, we're aware of our utter dependence upon him.

Humility arises from a biblical understanding of who we are and who God is, which leads to absolute submission to and absolute dependence upon God. "It is," says John Owen, "to humble our souls to the law of God's providence in all his dispensations—to fall down before his sovereignty, wisdom, righteousness, goodness, love, and mercy."[5] This is likely what Paul means when he writes, "I have learned in whatever situation I am to be content" (Philippians 4:11). He had to learn to be content, because it went against his nature—pride. Likewise, we must "learn" to subdue and humble our heart. When we do, the result is contentment—an indispensable quality when it comes to waiting confidently and expectantly for what God has promised.

## Calming and Quieting the Soul (v. 2)

"But I have calmed and quieted my soul, like a weaned child with its mother; like a weaned child is my soul within me."

Why does David's soul need calming and quieting? Perhaps he struggles with inordinate longing (overvaluing something he wants), obstinate clinging (overvaluing something he has), distrustful worrying (undervaluing God's power), or ungrateful murmuring (undervaluing God's goodness). Whatever the case, he claims to have "calmed and quieted [his] soul, like a weaned child with its mother."

What's David's point? "The weaned infant," explains Thomas Manton, "challenges nothing, expects nothing, but what his mother will give him."[6] A weaned child is cut off from his mother's milk, implying he no longer receives what he expects. Similarly, David calms and quiets his soul by cultivating self-denial. He weakens his attachment to the world and learns to esteem things according to their true value. Moreover, a weaned child is reliant upon his mother for everything, and he rests in his mother's provision. Similarly, David calms and quiets his soul by cultivating dependence, recognizing that all things come from God. Finally, a weaned child is happy with what his mother gives him. In other words, he's satisfied with small things. Similarly, David calms and quiets his soul by cultivating contentment and learns to live by what God gives him.

This picture of a weaned child is similar to the one Christ provides in Matthew 18. The disciples want to know who is the greatest in the kingdom of heaven (v. 1). We don't know what precipitates this, but we do know what's at the root of it—pride. Christ responds by placing a child in their midst and declaring, "Truly, I say to you, unless you turn and become like children, you will never enter the kingdom of heaven" (v. 3). What does he mean? To answer that question, we must be careful to distinguish between being *childish* and *childlike*. To be *childish* is to be immature. The Bible warns us not to be *childish* in the way we think or behave (Matthew 11:16; 1 Corinthians 14:20;

Ephesians 4:14). Therefore, when Christ says we must "become like children," he most certainly isn't saying we should be *childish*. He's affirming that we should be *childlike*. How? He tells us: "Whosoever humbles himself like this child is the greatest in the kingdom of heaven" (v. 4). Here, Christ calls his disciples' attention to the fact that children are completely dependent upon adults for survival. By extension, he's telling them that they must rid themselves of any desire for greatness and admit their childlike dependence upon God for all things. That is to say, they must humble themselves.

We must fix our mind on this singular truth: God—who is infinitely wise, incomparably powerful, and immeasurably good—is a Father who loves us and knows what's best for us. We calm and quiet our heart when we resign ourselves to his will with respect to present conditions and future events.

## Conclusion

"O Israel, hope in the LORD from this time forth and forevermore" (v. 3).

We can't hope unless we come to terms with two truths. When it comes to our pride, we need a subdued and humbled heart. When it comes to God's providence, we need a calmed and quieted soul. When these are in place, hope anchors our soul even when we pass through the deep waters of affliction.

> Will your anchor hold in the storms of life,
> when the clouds unfold their wings of strife?
> When the strong tides lift, and the cables strain,
> will your anchor drift or firm remain?
> We have an anchor that keeps the soul,
> steadfast and sure while the billows roll,
> Fastened to the Rock which cannot move,
> grounded firm and deep in the Savior's love.[7]

I began this chapter by affirming that hope is crucial to our journey homeward. How so? Paul thanks God for the church at Colossae because he has heard of their faith in Christ and love for the saints

(Colossians 1:4). In this prayer of thanksgiving, we have a sure test of spiritual growth. It isn't intellectual knowledge; just because we can unravel complex theological motifs doesn't mean we're growing spiritually. It isn't exceptional experiences, glamorous gifts, or marvelous ministries. The test of spiritual growth is vibrant faith (the object of which is God's Son) and vibrant love (the object of which is God's people). Interestingly, Paul goes on to say that the believers at Colossae are growing in faith and love "because of the hope laid up for [them] in heaven" (v. 5). In other words, "the hope of glory" (v. 27) is the fuel that causes their faith and love to burn bright.

How does hope strengthen faith? Difficult circumstances can weaken our faith; we become discouraged by the condition of this world, the sin in our hearts, the problems we encounter, and the losses we experience. But our hope is fixed on what will be: the return of Christ, the resurrection of the dead, and the renovation of the entire cosmos. Our hope makes this future certainty a present reality, thereby fueling our faith in Christ.

How does hope strengthen love? Difficult relationships can weaken our love; we become discouraged by the way people treat us and by the strain that marks so many of our relationships. But our hope is fixed on what will be: the day when all of God's people will be free from sin, when we'll be free from strife and contention, and when love will reign supreme. Our hope makes this future certainty a present reality, thereby fueling our love for others.

We abound in faith and love as we live in the certain expectation that God will fulfill all his promises.

## Questions

1. What is hope? How does this differ from the world's understanding of the term?

2. What are the two greatest impediments to hope? Do you struggle with these? How so?

3. Why is hope so important to our walk as Christians?

4. How do we subdue pride?

5. Are you ever agitated? If so, why?

6.  How does the psalmist calm his soul? How does this apply to your current circumstances?

7.  How does hope strengthen faith and love?

8.  How can you turn this psalm into a prayer? List specific requests.

# 13

# Nurturing Faith

## *Psalm 132*

[1] Remember, O LORD, in David's favor, all the hardships he endured,
[2] how he swore to the LORD and vowed to the Mighty One of Jacob,
[3] "I will not enter my house or get into my bed,
[4] I will not give sleep to my eyes or slumber to my eyelids,
[5] until I find a place for the LORD, a dwelling place for the Mighty One of Jacob."
[6] Behold, we heard of it in Ephrathah; we found it in the fields of Jaar.
[7] "Let us go to his dwelling place; let us worship at his footstool!"
[8] Arise, O LORD, and go to your resting place, you and the ark of your might.
[9] Let your priests be clothed with righteousness, and let your saints shout for joy.
[10] For the sake of your servant David, do not turn away the face of your anointed one.
[11] The LORD swore to David a sure oath from which he will not turn back:
"One of the sons of your body I will set on your throne.
[12] If your sons keep my covenant and my testimonies that I shall teach them,
their sons also forever shall sit on your throne."
[13] For the LORD has chosen Zion; he has desired it for his dwelling place:
[14] "This is my resting place forever; here I will dwell, for I have desired it.

[15] I will abundantly bless her provisions; I will satisfy her poor with bread.

[16] Her priests I will clothe with salvation, and her saints will shout for joy.

[17] There I will make a horn to sprout for David; I have prepared a lamp for my anointed.

[18] His enemies I will clothe with shame, but on him his crown will shine."

"The best-laid plans of mice and men go oft awry."[1] That's a famous line from a 1785 poem by Robert Burns, "To a Mouse, on Turning Her Up in Her Nest with the Plough." Apparently, Burns wrote the poem after destroying a mouse's nest while plowing his field. Later, he reflected upon the unfortunate incident: the mouse had expended so much time and effort in building a nest that was destroyed in the blink of an eye, and it was powerless to do anything about it. For Burns, the similarity between the mouse's plight and man's plight was striking. Whether we're a man or a mouse—great or small—our plans are subject to forces and factors beyond our control.

Let's imagine for a moment that I'm planning a picnic for this Saturday. My plan is contingent upon the weather; if it rains, my picnic will be ruined. My plan is also contingent upon my guests; if they choose not to attend, my picnic will be canceled. My plan is also contingent upon my car, if it breaks down my picnic will be delayed. Whenever we plan something, there are innumerable contingencies. "The best-laid plans of mice and men go oft awry."

But when it comes to God's plan, there are no contingencies. Why? There are no forces or factors beyond his control. His plan rests upon his unrivaled power, unfathomable knowledge, and unsearchable wisdom. This extremely encouraging truth means that all of God's promises come to pass. God is immutable, therefore his plans and promises are unchanging. This reality makes God the only suitable object where we can rest our faith.

Now, what is faith? According to popular portrayals, it's a really strong *feeling* that anything can happen. But despite its broad appeal, this definition has nothing to do with Scripture. Faith is simply the conviction that God's Word is true. When we believe God's Word is true, we comprehend realities that are above the reach of sense and reason. The author of Hebrews points to the creation of the universe as an example of faith (Hebrews 11:3). Without faith, man's understanding of the origin of the universe is nonsensical. For example, many people think the universe is self-created; in other words, they truly believe it came into existence by itself. This view is a logical absurdity because it affirms that *nothing* produced *something*, which violates the law of noncontradiction. How can something exist before it was? It can't. Faith alone allows understanding regarding the origin of the universe, as it takes to heart what God says in his Word. By faith, therefore, we gain insight into the origin of the universe: God created it by his word out of nothing.

Just as faith imparts certainty about what God says concerning the past, even so it also imparts certainty about what God says concerning the future. To put it another way, faith is the conviction that whatever God has promised will happen. It gives God's promises *substance* in the present by making them a present reality.

That's what we're going to see in Psalm 132, by far the longest of the Psalms of Ascent. My goal isn't to mine every detail but to provide an overall understanding of its central message by focusing on its setting and structure, followed by its scope and significance.

### Setting and Structure

"Arise, O LORD, and go to your resting place, you and the ark of your might. Let your priests be clothed with righteousness, and let your saints shout for joy. For the sake of your servant David, do not turn away the face of your anointed one" (vv. 8–10).

Here, the psalmist makes three prayer requests: he asks God to inhabit his "resting place," bless his "priests" and "saints," and preserve his "anointed." This prayer is important for a number of reasons, but for now, I simply want you to notice that it unlocks the psalm's historical setting since Solomon quotes this in 2 Chronicles 6:41–42. In that passage, Solomon has just finished building the temple in Jerusalem, and he utters this prayer at its dedication ceremony. Solo-

mon—who likely wrote the entire psalm—gives two reasons why
God should answer his prayer: David's devotion (vv. 1–7) and God's
covenant (vv. 11–18).

In the first seven verses, Solomon reminds God and his listeners
of David's devotion. "Remember, O LORD, in David's favor all the
hardships he endured" (v. 1). The historical context for this appeal
is 2 Samuel 6–7, where we learn that David brought the ark of the
covenant to the city of Jerusalem with great celebration. But he longed
to do more; he was disturbed that the ark stood in a tent while he
lived in luxury. He determined to build a temple to house the ark and
swore to God that he wouldn't rest until it's done (vv. 3–4). Here, he's
likely speaking by way of hyperbole in order to emphasize his zeal
for this cause. But God rejects David's plans and informs him that
his son, Solomon, will build the temple. At the temple's dedication
ceremony, Solomon appeals to David's devotion as a reason why God
should hear his prayer.

Second, Solomon appeals to God's covenant (vv. 11–18). "The
LORD swore to David a sure oath from which he will not turn back"
(v. 11). The historical context for this appeal is 2 Samuel 7. After
God rejected David's plan to build the temple, he proceeds to make
a covenant with David, promising to establish his son's kingdom
forever: "One of the sons of your body I will set on your throne" (v.
11). And so, at the temple's dedication ceremony, Solomon appeals
to God's covenant as another reason why God should hear his prayer.

### Scope and Significance

God answers Solomon's prayer. He does indeed inhabit his temple,
bless his people, and preserve his anointed—Solomon. But there's
something far more significant going on here than the immediate
fulfillment of Solomon's prayer in his day, and we dare not miss this
small detail in God's covenant: "If your sons keep my covenant and
my testimonies that I shall teach them, their sons also forever shall
sit on your throne" (v. 12; 2 Samuel 7:12–16). Here, God promises
that David's son will sit on his throne forever—*if* he keeps God's

covenant. In other words, the fulfillment of God's promise is contingent upon obedience.

Now, this detail raises a slight contingency problem: Solomon didn't keep God's covenant. As a matter of fact, he failed miserably. By the end of his reign, he had built shrines and temples for a host of false gods, and as a result, his son, Rehoboam, lost half the kingdom. The northern kingdom under Jeroboam plunged headlong into idolatry, which continued for several centuries until God sent the Assyrians to sweep it away in 722 BC. The southern kingdom lasted a little longer as there were a few good leaders among Solomon's physical descendants. For the most part, however, they too failed miserably, and consequently, in 586 BC, God sent the Babylonians to sweep it away.

These historical events lead to an obvious question: What happened to God's covenant with David? What happened to his promise to establish one of the sons of David's "body" on his throne? Here's what we must understand: when God established his covenant with David and made it conditional upon obedience, he had a specific man in view. *See Travel Tip #2.* It's the same man he had in view when he made his promise to Abraham (Genesis 17). It's the same man he had in view when he made his promise to Adam (Genesis 3). God has always had one man in view: Christ. As David's descendant, Christ obeyed God, and God established Christ upon David's throne, thereby fulfilling his promise. We hear this promise confirmed in the angel's proclamation to Mary: "He will be great and will be called the Son of the Most High. And the Lord God will give to him the throne of his father David, and he will reign over the house of Jacob forever, and of his kingdom there will be no end" (Luke 1:32).

Understanding this is extremely important because it means we must move beyond the immediate fulfillment of Solomon's prayer to its full and final fulfillment in Christ. Let's see how this works out in terms of Solomon's three requests. Solomon prayed: "Arise, O LORD, and go to your resting place" (v. 8). God has answered this prayer; he does indeed inhabit his temple. "In [Christ] all the fullness of God was pleased to dwell" (Colossians 1:19). By virtue of our union with Christ, we're "being built together into a dwelling place for God by the Spirit" (Ephesians 2:22). "For the LORD has chosen Zion; he has desired it for his dwelling place: 'This is my resting place forever; here I will dwell, for I have desired it'" (vv. 13–14).

Solomon prayed: "Let your priests be clothed with righteousness, and let your saints shout for joy" (v. 9). God has answered this prayer; he does indeed bless his people by making us one with Christ, whereby all that's his becomes ours. Our union with Christ is how God communicates all of his graces to us: "[we] have been filled in him" (Colossians 2:10). "I will abundantly bless her provisions; I will satisfy her poor with bread. Her priests I will clothe with salvation, and her saints will shout for joy" (vv. 15–16).

Solomon prayed: "Do not turn away the face of your anointed one" (v. 10). God has answered this prayer; he does indeed preserve his anointed. Paul, in his sermon recorded in Acts 13:32–39, quotes from Psalm 2, which begins with a description of those who oppose God's anointed. God responds to their opposition by laughing and scoffing at them, declaring that he has installed his king in Zion: "You are my Son, today I have begotten you." In his sermon, Paul affirms that this psalm is fulfilled in Christ's resurrection and ascension. God has set his Son upon David's throne. "There I will make a horn to sprout for David; I have prepared a lamp for my anointed. His enemies I will clothe with shame, but on him his crown will shine" (vv. 17–18).

Christ has inaugurated his kingdom. *See Travel Tip #2.* It isn't identified with any particular country, aligned with any political party, or defined by any social institution. It's his rule over his people, meaning it's relational, and to be in the kingdom is to be in a right relationship with the King. We don't see Christ's kingdom at present, but we will. We don't see the renovation of all things in him just yet, but we will. We don't see the subjugation of all kingdoms to him just yet, but we will. We're awaiting the consummation of the kingdom. One day, the present kingdom of grace will give way to the future kingdom of glory. Creation will be renewed, and paradise will be restored. There will be no sound of weeping and no cry of distress. There will be no tension, division, turmoil, conflict, or death. The earth will be filled with the knowledge of God's glory, which will shine in every crevice and upon every creature. A renewed heaven and earth will be occupied by a multitude of glorified people, and the King will dwell in their midst forever.

## Conclusion

When we see the full panorama of this psalm, we begin to recognize several revitalizing truths. To begin with, it shows us that God's promise doesn't change. David figures prominently throughout the psalm: "Remember, O LORD, in David's favor" (v. 1); "For the sake of your servant David" (v. 10); "The LORD swore to David a sure oath from which he will not turn back" (v. 11); "There I will make a horn to sprout for David" (v. 17). Why is there so much emphasis on David? It's simple: God's covenant with David forms the foundation of Solomon's confidence in this prayer. To put it another way, all that Solomon asks is for David's sake. Similarly, God's covenant should form the foundation of our confidence and assurance in prayer. All that we ask is for Christ's sake.

When I was a young boy, my mother taught me to pray: "As I lay me down to sleep, I pray the Lord my soul to keep. If I die before I wake, take me to heaven for Jesus' sake." The phrase—"If I die before I wake"—was a little troubling for a four-year-old boy to ponder just before turning off the lights, but that's a topic for another time. For now, I'm interested in the phrase: "Take me to heaven for Jesus' sake." It's beautiful, because it articulates so well for young and old the essence of the gospel and the object of our faith. *See Travel Tip #1*. God remembers us for Christ's sake: he remembers Christ's humility, not our pride; he remembers Christ's righteousness, not our unrighteousness; he remembers Christ's obedience, not our disobedience; he remembers Christ's faithfulness, not our unfaithfulness; he remembers Christ's devotion, not our apathy; and he remembers Christ's love, not our cold heart. It's all for Christ's sake.

Our faith is fixed on God's covenant—his sure promise in Christ. The Old Testament saints didn't receive what was promised (Hebrews 11:39); although they longed for its fulfillment (Luke 10:24; 1 Peter 1:10–11), they never enjoyed it as we do. Why not? A. W. Pink explains, "It is at this point, and no other, we find the essential difference between the faith of the Old Testament saints and the faith of the New Testament saints: the one looked forward to a Saviour that was to come, the other looks back to a Saviour who has come."[2] We have a better view of Christ than the Old Testament saints ever had; they had the shadow, but we have the substance. Therefore, we have a better object of faith than they ever had; they had what Christ would accomplish, but we have what Christ has accomplished.

Our faith is rooted in the accomplishment of God's promises in the past; that is, it's rooted in God's saving acts in human history, culminating in the incarnation of his Son. Our faith is also fixed on the certain accomplishment of God's promises in the future. *See Travel Tip #3.* Our faith embraces our eschatological hope: the return of Christ, the resurrection of the dead, the final judgment, the renovation of the universe, and the consummation of all things. Our faith gives these promises *substance* in the present, whereby they shape our journey home.

## Questions

1. Do you struggle with spiritual weariness? If so, why?
2. How do you respond when God's answer to your prayer is *not yet*?
3. What is biblical faith?
4. Explain the relationship between God's unchangeableness and faithfulness?
5. What is the object of our faith?
6. God's steadfast love is life (Ps. 119:88). Explain.
7. How can you turn this psalm into a prayer? List specific requests.

# 14

# Maintaining Unity

## *Psalm 133*

[1] Behold, how good and pleasant it is when brothers dwell in unity!
[2] It is like the precious oil on the head, running down on the beard,
on the beard of Aaron,
running down on the collar of his robes!
[3] It is like the dew of Hermon, which falls on the mountains of Zion!
For there the LORD has commanded the blessing, life forevermore.

"Next to communion with God," writes George Swinnock, "there is no communion like the communion of saints."[1] As we make the long and difficult journey home, God uses this "communion," or Christian fellowship, to comfort the discouraged, recover the wayward, challenge the careless, encourage the sorrowful, orient the confused, and revive the exhausted. In other words, God uses Christian fellowship to impart grace to the travel-weary soul. It sounds wonderful, doesn't it? Then why does it also sound so different than what many of us experience in the context of the church? Imagine this all-too-familiar scene from an unknown source:

> A church was in the midst of its monthly business meeting. The finances were in better shape than usual, so the moderator asked if there were any special needs. One lady stood and slowly proceeded to explain that she felt the church needed a better chandelier.

Before she was finished, a deacon jumped to his feet and shouted, "I'm against it for three reasons. Nobody knows how to spell it. Nobody knows how to play it. And what this church really needs is better lighting."

You can envision the chaos that ensued. Sadly, scenes such as that have been repeated on innumerable occasions throughout the church's history. Two groups or individuals within a local church disagree over something, and soon they're on a collision course; lines are drawn, walls are built, and trenches are dug. The only two possible results are a cold war whereby the two sides avoid each other or a civil war whereby the two sides tear each other apart. "Next to communion with God, there is no communion like the communion of saints." Yeah, right!

If you're dubious, here's what you must grasp: even scenes like the ones just described don't alter the reality of the blessing that flows from true Christian fellowship. They do, however, remind us of our calling to be "eager to maintain the unity of the Spirit in the bond of peace" (Ephesians 4:3). We'll get to *how* we maintain unity shortly, but first let's focus on *why* we ought to be "eager" to do so. And that brings us to Psalm 133.

## The Nature of Unity (v. 1)

"Behold, how good and pleasant it is when brothers dwell in unity!"

David's choice of words is intriguing: "good and pleasant." Some things are good but unpleasant. Medicine, for example, is helpful for treating a sore throat, but it tastes terrible. On the other hand, some things are pleasant but not good. Fried food tastes great (I think so, anyway), but too much of it can lead to serious health problems. Even if those are not the best examples, I'm sure you get the basic idea: unity is both *good* and *pleasant*. Why? The answer emerges in the next couple of verses.

## The Origin of Unity (vv. 2–3)

"It is like the precious oil on the head, running down on the beard, on the beard of Aaron, running down on the collar of his robes! It is like the dew of Hermon, which falls on the mountains of Zion!"

Here, David uses two word pictures. The first is the oil on Aaron's head, which is a difficult image for most of us to appreciate. I get chills just thinking about this—oil running down my head in between my neck and shirt collar; it's bad enough at the barber's when clipped hair gets down in there. But it's important that we don't let the imagery cause us to lose sight of the symbolism in these verses. This anointing of the high priest's head with olive oil mixed with the best spices was a sign of consecration (Exodus 30:22–33). As the oil ran down from the high priest's head to his robes, it emitted a pleasant aroma. David says unity is like rich perfume—it's pleasant.

The second word picture is the dew on Hermon, a mountain located in northern Israel, which is known for its plentiful moisture. Obviously, an abundance of moisture means an abundance of vegetation. David says unity leads to fruitfulness—it's good.

The detail I want you to notice is that both word pictures point to the origin of the blessing. David uses the phrase "running down" in reference to the oil on Aaron's head, and he uses the phrase "falls on" in reference to the dew on Hermon's mount. These phrases emphasize descent. The point is that the blessing of unity descends from above; it comes from God.

## The Blessing of Unity (v. 3)

"For there the LORD has commanded the blessing, life forevermore."

What does David mean by "there"? The answer is found in the last word of the preceding verse: Zion. David is saying that God has "commanded the blessing"—unity—at Jerusalem. This detail sheds some light on this psalm's historical context. David is very likely pointing to his ascension to the throne of Israel as the catalyst for the unity he celebrates.

After entering the land of Canaan, Israel experienced one of the most turbulent periods in its history: the days of the judges. During these centuries, Israel existed as a loose confederation of tribes, plagued by inner turmoil and moral, social, political, and religious chaos. Why? "In those days there was no king in Israel. Everyone did what was right in his own eyes" (Judges 21:25). This widespread unrest continued through the reign of the first king, Saul. After Saul's death, David became king of Judah, while Ish-bosheth, Saul's son, became king of the other tribes, a division that led to a brutal civil war (2 Samuel 2). After defeating Ish-bosheth, David was able to unite all of the tribes under his rule: "Then all the tribes of Israel came to David at Hebron and said, 'Behold, we are your bone and flesh'" (2 Samuel 5:1).

In all likelihood, David has this momentous event in mind in Psalm 133. After centuries of disunity, Israel is finally united under his rule, and God has orchestrated this blessing (v. 3). It's like the precious oil, running down on Aaron's beard (v. 2) or the dew of Hermon, falling on the mountains of Zion (v. 3). David's cry is the culmination of the nation's long and arduous journey to this era of unprecedented blessing: "Behold, how good and pleasant it is when brothers dwell in unity!"

## A Greater Unity

But David's celebration is relatively short-lived. Soon after Solomon's death, the old divisions resurface, the kingdom splits in two, and both eventually fall to foreign invaders. At first glance, this rapid change in events makes David's exuberant celebration seem pointless and meaningless. Or, does it? In grappling with this idea, it's important to remember that we interpret these psalms through the lens of Christ and his mediatorial kingdom. *See Travel Tip #2.* In the context of Psalm 133, we see the fulfillment of David's celebration in Christ: we affirm that God has "commanded the blessing" at Zion by establishing a far greater unity in Christ.

God is a relational being—Father, Son, and Spirit—and he made us relational beings, creating us to be in relation with him and others. However, our relationship with God and one another suffered the negative consequences of Adam's sin, and we have lived with the relational breakdown ever since. But Christ has established a new humanity—a new creation—having made peace by the blood of his cross (Ephesians 2:13–16). God saves us by making us one with Christ by the Holy Spirit. This union links redemption *accomplished* and redemption *applied*, meaning all that Christ purchased for us flows to us by virtue of our union with him. When God makes us one with Christ, he also makes us one with each other, and we become members of the church—the body and bride of Christ. As such, we become Christ's visible form in the world, reflecting his splendor, manifesting his glory, displaying his beauty, and mirroring his holiness.

This unity is one of the reasons Paul describes the church as a body: "We are to grow up in every way into him who is the head, into Christ, from whom the whole body, joined and held together by every joint with which it is equipped, when each part is working properly, makes the body grow so that it builds itself up in love" (Ephesians 4:15–16). Our physical body is an amazing thing. It's comprised of a series of joints—each consisting of two smooth bones, fit together perfectly, and working together effortlessly and harmoniously. Joining these bones are ligaments—tightly bound fibers. Joining bones to muscles are tendons—more tightly bound fibers. Running throughout our physical body is a cardiovascular system: the heart pumping blood through an elaborate system of veins and arteries. We also possess a nervous system that connects the smallest nerve in my fingertip through my arm into my spinal cord, where it's connected by strands of nerves to my brain. I initiate movement by willing it in my brain, which sends out energy that passes through my nervous system, which then moves my arm, hand, and fingers.

Paul says the church is much like our physical body, and that by virtue of our union with Christ, we're knit together like joints, ligaments, and tendons in his spiritual body. When each of us functions properly, the body "builds itself up in love." This is the "blessing" that God has "commanded" at Zion (v. 3). It's like the oil, running down on Aaron's beard (v. 2). It's like the dew, falling on the mountains of Zion (v. 3). "Behold, how good and pleasant it is when brothers dwell in unity!"

## Conclusion

Given the tremendous blessing that flows from unity, we should be eager to protect and preserve it. As I write this, my right hand is tingling, my fingers are numb, and I'm experiencing throbbing pain from my right shoulder to my right elbow. According to the MRI, the disk between the C-6 and C-7 vertebrae in my neck is bulging and pinching the nerve. Because one little part of my body isn't functioning properly, the rest of my body suffers. The same thing occurs within the body of Christ when one part doesn't function properly. Although our unity can never be destroyed, it can easily be disturbed; hence Paul's admonition to "maintain the unity of the Spirit in the bond of peace" (Ephesians 4:3).

But what exactly does this look like? We maintain unity by promoting truth: "I appeal to you, brothers, by the name of our Lord Jesus Christ, that all of you agree and that there be no divisions among you, but that you be united in the same mind and the same judgment" (1 Corinthians 1:10). Unity is based on a common confession. This is one of the reasons why creeds and confessions are so important; we can't confess something that's nebulous. At times, however, it's difficult to balance our call to proclaim truth with our call to love one another. To what point does truth trump love, or love trump truth? John Stott provides a thoughtful response: "In fundamentals, faith is primary, and we may not appeal to love as an excuse to deny essential truth. In non-fundamentals, however, love is primary, and we may not appeal to zeal for the faith as an excuse for failures in love."[2] We aren't to tolerate moral or doctrinal evil in our midst, but neither are we to tolerate disputes which arise from envy, bitterness, and misunderstanding. We must actively seek peace within the body, recognizing that we're one. Every decision should be based in large measure upon what brings peace to the church without compromising the truth.

We also maintain unity by cultivating humility: "For by the grace given to me I say to everyone among you not to think of himself more highly than he ought to think, but to think with sober judgment" (Romans 12:3). Because we want to be uppermost, there's conflict. Because we want our own way, there's conflict. Because we long to be noticed, valued, and esteemed, there's conflict. Because we're driven by self-love, there's conflict.

Pride makes us want to be in control, causing anxiety. It makes us think we deserve better, causing discouragement. It makes us think we've been unfairly treated, causing bitterness. It makes us wish people would notice us, causing discontentment. It makes us desire to be uppermost, causing envy and malice. Do we recognize these truths about ourselves? Recognizing them, do we strive to think of ourselves with "sober judgment"?

Thinking soberly provides a proper self-perspective before God. Just as "the stars vanish when the sun appears,"[3] a sight of God's glory humbles. We're weak in comparison to his power, foolish in comparison to his wisdom, ignorant in comparison to his knowledge, and feeble in comparison to his sovereignty. When we compare ourselves to God's excellence, we see our smallness. We grasp that our "exceptional strength, intelligence, wisdom, or beauty, are merely superiorly arranged dust, and God did the arranging."[4]

Another way to maintain unity is to make peace: "Blessed are the peacemakers, for they shall be called the sons of God" (Matthew 5:9). What does it mean to be a peacemaker? William Perkins explains, "Where God's Spirit works peace of conscience towards God in Christ, there the same Spirit does move the party to seek peace with all men; as also to make peace between those that are at variance."[5] Those who are proud, discontented, and resentful cause discord wherever they go; however, those who are at peace with God keep the peace, seeking to extinguish anger, strife, and division. Perhaps one of our greatest callings isn't to make peace where there's trouble, but simply to refrain from making trouble where there's peace. "For lack of wood the fire goes out, and where there is no whisperer, quarreling ceases" (Proverbs 26:20). "A significant portion of peacemaking," says Terry Johnson, "has to do not with actively doing anything, but with just leaving things alone. A peacemaker often need not actually take positive action, but merely refrain from disturbing the peace."[6]

Finally, and most importantly, we maintain unity by nurturing love: "And above all these put on love which binds everything together in perfect harmony" (Colossians 3:14). A. W. Pink comments, "Brotherly love is a tender plant which requires much attention: if it be not watched and watered, it quickly wilts."[7] We "watch and water" brotherly love by camping at the foot of the cross. God set his love upon us before the foundation of the world and demonstrated his love for us by sending his Son to die for us. He poured out his love within our heart by sending his Spirit to dwell in us, and his love compels us to love.

In large part, maintaining unity entails believing the gospel—the power of God for salvation (Romans 1:16). Do we really believe that God changes people through the gospel, that he transforms people through the gospel, and that he shapes, nurtures, teaches, and matures people through the gospel? If we do, the gospel will determine how we approach others, receive others, view others, and love others. The gospel puts us on a level playing field because it robs us of any motive for pride. According to James Boice:

> Christ is served when we understand that we are accepted by God through the work of Christ alone and are therefore able joyfully to accept and love all others for whom Christ died. These other believers may be wrong in many respects, in our opinion. But we will know that we are all nevertheless part of one spiritual body, the body of Christ, and that we belong together as we seek to live for Christ.[8]

## Questions

1. What is Christian communion?
2. Are you a member of a local church? Are you involved?
3. Why is Christian fellowship important?
4. How is the church like a physical body? See Eph. 4:15–16.
5. Do you struggle to get along with other Christians? How can you maintain unity?
6. Why is the gospel fundamental to unity?
7. How might the church be equipped to minister to you in your present circumstances?
8. Identify one person in your church in need of edifying or encouraging or comforting. Consider how God might use you to fulfill this need.
9. How can you turn this psalm into a prayer? List specific requests.

# 15

# Blessing God

## *Psalm 134*

¹ Come, bless the LORD, all you servants of the LORD,
who stand by night in the house of the LORD!
² Lift up your hands to the holy place and bless the LORD!
³ May the LORD bless you from Zion, he who made heaven and earth!

We've arrived at the end of our journey through the Psalms of Ascent. Along the way, we've followed psalmists as they travel from the depths of pain to the heights of joy, from the depths of despair to the heights of jubilation, from the depths of doubt to the heights of assurance, from the depths of guilt to the heights of forgiveness, from the depths of bondage to the heights of deliverance. Through it all, one thing has remained constant: the psalmists never take their eyes off God.

If we're struggling with discouragement arising from affliction, looking to God will strengthen us. If we're struggling with destructive patterns in our thinking and living, looking to God will cause us to forsake our sin. If we're struggling with pride, envy, or bitterness, looking to God will cultivate poverty of spirit within us. If we're struggling to forgive those who've hurt us, looking to God will cause us to weep on their behalf. If we're struggling with the call to deny self, looking to God will make us willing to live for him. If we're struggling with addiction, looking to God will captivate our heart and satisfy our deepest longing. If we're struggling to resist the world's allurements, looking to God will turn our heart away from the world's unholy trinity of pleasure, profit, and power. If we're struggling with laziness and carelessness, looking to God will awaken us from our slumber. If we're struggling to come to grips with numerous uncertainties, looking to God will calm our greatest fears.

This overarching theme comes to a very fitting conclusion in Psalm 134, where the psalmist *blesses* God. If God is so great, then what praise, honor, and glory should we give to him? "Praise him according to his excellent greatness" (Psalm 150:2). We can't praise God to the utmost of his greatness, but we can praise him to the utmost of our ability. We can give him our highest praises: "Let the high praises of God be in their throats" (Psalm 149:6). And we can give him our greatest praises: "Great is the LORD, and greatly to be praised" (Psalm 145:3). We're unable to give him all the glory that's due his name, but we can give him all that our soul has to offer. "Bless the LORD, O my soul, and all that is within me, bless his holy name" (Psalm 103:1).

When it's all said and done, we bless what we esteem, and we esteem what we treasure. One of the principal themes in J. R. Tolkien's *The Hobbit* is treasure. The dwarves of Erebor—the Lonely Mountain—are consumed with it, and they amass a fortune in the mountain's deepest caverns. The dragon Smaug comes in search of the treasure, killing and destroying for it. He has no practical use for it, except to sleep in it. Thorin and his band of dwarves are prepared to sacrifice life and limb to reclaim the treasure from Smaug. After they succeed, humans and elves arrive on the scene demanding a share of the treasure, and they're prepared to go to war over it. What's Tolkien's point through all of this? It's simple: man is consumed by his pursuit of treasure.

Now, there's nothing wrong with the pursuit of treasure per se. The problem isn't our desire for treasure, but the object of our desire. Christ declares, "For where your treasure is, there your heart will be also" (Matthew 6:21). His point is that we inevitably move toward our treasure—whatever captures our hearts. For this reason, John Flavel warns, "Look what is highest in the estimation, first and last in the thoughts, and upon which we spend our time and strength with delight; certainly, that is our treasure."[1]

We bless what we esteem, and we esteem what we treasure. As made evident throughout these psalms, the psalmists treasure the one who is enthroned in the heavens. This becomes readily apparent in Psalm 134. It's likely this psalm was penned for the Israelites to sing upon arriving at or departing from the city of Jerusalem. In verses 1–2, they call out to the priests to bless God. In verse 3, the priests respond by announcing God's blessing.

## A Call to Worship (vv. 1–2)

"Come, bless the LORD, all you servants of the LORD, who stand by night in the house of the LORD! Lift up your hands to the holy place and bless the LORD!"

Here, the people encourage the priests ("all you servants of the LORD") to bless God. The psalmist doesn't mention why, but it isn't difficult to fill in the details: God, who's enthroned in the heavens (Psalm 123:1), is the Maker of heaven and earth (Psalm 121:2; 124:8; 134:3).

The prophet Isaiah was privileged to see a vision of this great God, telling us he saw "the Lord sitting upon a throne, high and lifted up" (Isaiah 6:1). Here, the term "Lord" is *Adonai*—the plural form of *Adon*. It's used to describe the relationship between husband and wife; Sarah refers to Abraham as her *adon* (Genesis 18). It's also used to describe the relationship between master and slave; Eliezer refers to Abraham as his *adon* (Genesis 24). When ascribed to God, therefore, the title *Adonai* reveals that God is the supreme Lord and Master: "For the LORD your God is God of gods and Lord of lords, the great, the mighty, and the awesome God" (Deuteronomy 10:17).

As Isaiah gazed upon the Lord on his throne, he noticed that "the train of his robe filled the temple." Whenever I read this description, I think of walking into what was called "the old arena" in Markham, Ontario, where I grew up. At one end of the rink, there was an enormous portrait of Queen Elizabeth on the wall, which was a little unsettling since it was impossible to escape her gaze anywhere on the ice. In this particular portrait, the train of the queen's robe covered the stairs in front of her because since ancient times, the train of a monarch's robe has been a symbol of grandeur: the larger the train, the greater the grandeur. In the portrait Isaiah paints, the train of God's robe doesn't merely cover a few stairs or an entire staircase. It actually fills the temple, thereby symbolizing his incomparable grandeur.

Isaiah also saw the seraphim standing above the Lord: "Each had six wings: with two he covered his face, and with two he covered his feet, and with two he flew" (Isaiah 6:2). The vision of the seraphim covering their faces with two of their wings reminds us of the time in Moses' life when he asks to see God's glory. God responds, "You cannot see my face, for man shall not see me and live" (Exodus 33:20). Moses can't see God because he's a sinner, and to see God's face is death. Interestingly, the seraphim aren't sinful creatures, yet even they can't look at God's face. His glory is too bright even for them, and so they cover their faces with two wings. But why do they cover their feet with two wings? This reminds us of another incident in Moses' life. When he approaches the burning bush in the wilderness, God speaks to him: "Do not come near; take your sandals off your feet, for the place on which you are standing is holy ground" (Exodus 3:5). Feet are a symbol of finitude. Moses is a finite creature in the presence of an infinite God, which is symbolized in the removal of his sandals. The seraphim are also creatures; therefore, they cover their feet with two wings.

The seraphim call to one another: "Holy, holy, holy, is the LORD of hosts; the whole earth is full of his glory" (Isaiah 6:3). The expression "Holy, holy, holy" is the superlative in Hebrew. It simply means that God is the holiest, and this is the most fundamental truth we can declare about him. God is holy primarily because he's blameless. He's morally pure and perfect. God is also holy in that he's incomparable: "The LORD is high above all nations, and his glory above the heavens! Who is like the LORD our God, who is seated on high?" (Psalm 113:4–5).

I want you to appreciate that this is the incomparable God whom the psalmist blesses. There's no proportion between this limitless God and our limited mind, between this boundless God and our bound intellect, between this infinite God and our finite understanding.[2] Those who hear him most clearly hear but a faint whisper. Those who see him most fully see but a small glimmer. Those who understand most about him understand nothing, considering what there is to be known. "He does great things and unsearchable, marvelous things without number" (Job 5:9). "Your way was through the sea; your path through the great waters; yet your footprints were unseen" (Psalm 77:19). "It is he who sits above the circle of the earth, and its inhabitants are like grasshoppers" (Isaiah 40:22). This is the God we're called to bless.

## A Benediction (v. 3)

"May the LORD bless you from Zion, he who made heaven and earth!"

How does God bless us from Zion? He gives himself to us. We find in him all we could ever want. We find an eternal and spiritual good, suitable to our every need. Our knowledge of this God diffuses into our soul a satisfying peace in this life and a tantalizing taste of what awaits us in glory. "Blessed are the people whose God is the LORD!" (Psalm 144:15). This infinite God peers into our heart—weighing its desires, motives, impulses, and inclinations, and sees our heart riddled with self-love. This sin is an affront to him—a transgression of his law, rejection of his rule, desecration of his goodness, and violation of his glory. He has power to avenge himself. With a mere look he can cast us into hell.

Amazingly, this incomparable God draws near in the incarnation. His Son fulfills the law's demands, bearing our sin and shame. He makes us one with his Son, thereby linking redemption accomplished and redemption applied. All the blessings of salvation that Christ purchased for us flow to us through our union with him. God forgives us of our guilt and cleanses us of our filth, in Christ. We live upon Christ's merit and commune with him in his names and titles, his righteousness and holiness, his death, burial, and resurrection.

His mercy defies apprehension: "Your steadfast love is great above the heavens" (Psalm 108:4). His mercy evokes admiration: "How precious is your steadfast love" (Psalm 36:7). God owns us as his people. He owns us by creation—he made us in his image. He owns us by election—he chose us before we were born. He owns us by redemption—he paid an infinite price for us. He owns us by regeneration—he caused us to be born again. He owns us by adoption—he made us part of his family. In a word, this incomparable God is our Father. That's how he blesses us from Zion.

## Conclusion

What manner of God is this? He knows no beginning, succession, or ending. He's from everlasting to everlasting. He's the cause of all things. Do we have any effect upon this God? Does he need us? Does he gain anything from us? He's a perfect being, meaning he's incapable of increase or decrease. Nothing can be added to him or subtracted from him. He doesn't require anything outside of himself, nor does he benefit from anything outside of himself. Our effect upon God is that of a snowball hurled at the blazing sun.

What are we to God? He's like a sphere whose center is everywhere and whose circumference is nowhere. He isn't shut in, or shut out, of any space. He isn't far from us, yet he's far above and beyond us. He "hangs the earth on nothing . . . He binds up the waters in his thick clouds . . . He covers the face of the full moon . . . He has inscribed . . . the boundary between light and darkness . . . Behold, these are but the outskirts of his ways, and how small a whisper do we hear of him" (Job 26:7–14).

This is the God we bless, and this is the God who blesses us. When we know this God, we enjoy a blessing which the greatest storm can't touch, a peace which the roughest sea can't upset, and a delight which the mightiest wind can't disturb.

When we bless this God, we travel well and we end well—no matter what we encounter on our way home.

## Questions
1. What does it mean to bless God?

2. In what sense is *praise* the great revealer of the heart? What does your praise reveal about you?

3. Whatever your circumstances, what reasons do you have for praising God?

4. Do you meditate regularly upon God's incomparableness?

5. Without meditation upon God's truth, our minds wander dangerously into a world of enticing thoughts, discouraging thoughts, embittering thoughts, and distracting thoughts. Do you agree? Do you see this tendency in your own life?

6. How does God bless us? How should this affect us? How does this speak to your present circumstances?

7. How can you turn this psalm into a prayer? List specific requests.

# Appendix
# God's Providence

God "works all things according to the counsel of his will" (Ephesians 1:11). I wish we could leave the subject of God's providence at that, but we can't for the simple reason that this all-encompassing view of God's providence perplexes a lot of people. It usually raises three questions.

**The First Question. Is God the Author of Evil?**

If he "works all things according to the counsel of his will," then he must be responsible for all things, including evil. Right? Wrong. The solution to this *apparent* conundrum is the doctrine of *concurrence*, whereby we affirm that in the production of every effect there's an efficiency of two causes: first and second. What does that mean? God (the first cause) decrees everything that comes to pass; however, he isn't responsible for evil because he moves second causes to act freely in accordance with their desires.

I realize this talk of first and second causes is a little tricky, so let me attempt to simplify it. Let's think in terms of an action such as eating, drinking, speaking, throwing, sitting, etc. In the performance of any action, there's *motion* and *motive*. Correct? An action's motion—in itself—is never evil. It's the motive (desire) behind the action that determines whether the action is good or bad. Here's an example. Is it sinful to speak? Think carefully. The motion of speaking is never sinful in itself, but the motive behind it might make it sinful. When Jacob claimed to be Esau, thereby deceiving his father, Isaac, he sinned (Genesis 27). It was his motive (corrupt desires) that made his speaking sinful. Here's another example. Is it sinful to drink? Again, the motion of drinking is never sinful in itself, but the motive behind it might make it sinful. When Noah became drunk from drinking too much wine, he sinned (Genesis 9). It was his motive (corrupt desires) that made his drinking sinful.

Does that make sense? Let's keep building. Who's responsible for an action's motion? The answer is God—the first cause: "In him we live and move and have our being" (Acts 17:28). Who's responsible for an action's motive? The answer is man—the second cause. This means that God is the first cause (motion), and man is the second cause (motive) of all actions. That's the doctrine of *concurrence*. Again, in the production of every effect, there's an efficiency of two causes: first and second. And that's how we affirm that nothing falls outside the parameters of God's control, while also maintaining that he isn't the author of evil.

## The Second Question. Does God Approve of Evil?

If he "works all things according to the counsel of his will," then he must in some way deem evil to be good. Right? Wrong. We handle this perplexing question by upholding the distinction between God's *secret* will and *revealed* will (Deuteronomy 29:29).[3] The first refers to the rule of God's actions (God's decrees), whereas the second refers to the rule of man's actions (God's precepts). While we can't fully reconcile the mechanics of these two wills, we recognize that Scripture does support such a distinction. (We haven't wandered into the realm of mere philosophical speculation.)

Joseph's brothers sinned when they sold him into slavery. This event wasn't God's revealed will (will of precept), but it was his secret will (will of decree). How do we know? Joseph declares to his brothers: "It was not you who sent me here, but God" (Genesis 45:8). The Jews sinned when they crucified Christ. Again, this event wasn't God's revealed will (will of precept), but it was his secret will (will of decree). How do we know? Peter declares, "This Jesus, delivered up according to the definite plan and foreknowledge of God, you crucified and killed by the hands of lawless men" (Acts 2:23).

By an act of his will, therefore, God decrees all things that come to pass. But he does so in two ways. By a *positive* decree, he wills that which is good; and he effects the good that he decrees. By a *privative* decree, he wills that which is evil; and he willingly permits the evil he decrees. This doesn't mean God approves of the evil that he willingly permits, because it's possible for something to happen according to God's secret will yet against his revealed will. When God willingly permits evil, he doesn't contradict his revealed will because he doesn't approve of it, but he approves of the good that he aims at in willingly permitting it.

### The Third Question. Do We Possess Free Will?

If God "works all things according to the counsel of his will," then free will must be a fallacy. Right? Wrong. This is one of the most complex and controversial issues in the history of the church. Towering theologians, such as Augustine, Martin Luther, John Calvin, John Owen, and Jonathan Edwards devoted a great deal of time to this subject, formulating definitions and engaging in controversies.

What's all the fuss about? Generally speaking, there are two main schools of thought on the nature of human free will: *indeterminism* and *determinism*. The first maintains that our will is free from internal motives and desires; in other words, it's free from our mind's thoughts and our heart's affections. That means it possesses arbitrary power: we don't know why it chooses what it chooses. The second school of thought maintains that our will isn't free from internal motives and desires; in other words, it isn't free from our mind's thoughts and our heart's affections. That means it doesn't possess arbitrary power: we do know why it chooses what it chooses.

We affirm the second (or, at least, I do). I affirm that people are free in the choices they make because they're free from external constraints and compulsions. But I also affirm that our free will is in bondage to our own corrupt faculties—our mind is darkened and our heart is hardened (Ephesians 4:18). Our will doesn't possess arbitrary power; on the contrary, it follows the dictates of misplaced affections. Now, this doesn't undermine self-determination because it maintains a difference between *constraining* and *nonconstraining* causes. We're free because our choices are our own, but our choices aren't free from our darkened mind and hardened heart. In a word, we possess a free will that's in bondage to sin.

Have you got all that? A brief summary of some of the complexities surrounding the doctrine of God's providence—a little presumptuous, I know. But, at the very least, I trust I've provided several important categories for understanding this great truth.

# Notes

**Preface**

1. As quoted by Timothy Keller, The Prodigal God: Recovering the Heart of the Christian Faith (New York: Penguin, 2008), 94–95.

2. This is the Latin translation (as found in the Vulgate) of Pilate's statement recorded in John 19:5. The English translation is: "Behold the man!"

3. Sam Jones, "Spanish Church Mural Ruined by Well-Intentioned Restorer," The Guardian (August 22, 2012), http://www.theguardian.com/artanddesign/2012/aug/22/spain-church-mural-ruin-restoration.

4. John Calvin, Commentary on the Book of Psalms, in Calvin's Commentaries, 22 vols. (Grand Rapids: Baker, 2003), 4:xxxvii.

**Introduction**

1. C. J. Mahaney, The Cross Centered Life: Keeping the Gospel the Main Thing (Sisters, OR: Multnomah, 2002), 18–19.

2. Thomas Adams, The Works of Thomas Adams (Edinburgh: James Nichol, 1861–1862), 3:224.

3. Jeremy Walker, "Christ in All the Scriptures and Jesus on Every Page, Reformation 21 (August 20, 2013), http://www.reformation21.org/blog/2013/08/christ-in-all-the-scriptures-a.php.

4. Don Carson, A Call to Spiritual Reformation: Priorities from Paul and His Prayers (Grand Rapids: Baker, 2005), 61.

**Chapter 1**

1. Edward Pearse, A Beam of Divine Glory; or, The Unchangeableness of God Opened, Vindicated, and Improved (1674; repr., Morgan: Soli Deo Gloria, 1998), 83.

2. Jonathan Edwards, The Most High: A Prayer-Hearing God, in The Works of Jonathan Edwards (Edinburgh: Banner of Truth, 1974), 2:116.

3. Calvin, Commentary on the Book of Psalms, 6:5.58.

**Chapter 2**

1. John Bunyan, The Pilgrim's Progress (Uhrichsville, OH: Barbour, 1985), 134.

2. J. B. Lightfoot, St. Paul's Epistles to the Colossians and Philemon (Peabody, MA: Hendrickson, 1999), 156.

3. Matthew Henry, Commentary on the Whole Bible, ed. Leslie F. Church (Grand Rapids: Zondervan, 1961), 715.

## Chapter 3

1. Kevin DeYoung, "Mad-Libbing Church Angst," The Gospel Coalition (June 30, 2009), http://thegospelcoalition.org/blogs/kevindeyoung/2009/page/19.

2. I am indebted to Anthony Selvaggio for his insights on this subject in Seven Toxic Ideas Polluting Your Mind (Phillipsburg, NJ: P&R, 2011).

3. Selvaggio, Seven Toxic Ideas, 61.

4. Carl Trueman, The Creedal Imperative (Wheaton, IL: Crossway, 2012), 27.

5. Trueman, Creedal Imperative, 28.

6. For a full treatment of this trend, see David Wells, No Place for Truth; or, Whatever Happened to Evangelical Theology? (Grand Rapids: Eerdmans, 1994), 137–250.

7. Calvin, Commentary on the Book of Psalms, 6:5.74.

8. Samuel Stone, "The Church's One Foundation," 1866.

9. Jeremy Walker, Life in Christ: Becoming and Being a Disciple of the Lord Jesus Christ (Grand Rapids: Reformation Heritage Books, 2013), 107.

## Chapter 4

1. David Wells, God in the Wasteland: The Reality of Truth in a World of Fading Dreams (Grand Rapids: Eerdmans, 1994), 29.

2. Richard Baxter, A Christian Directory, in The Practical Works of Richard Baxter, 4 vols. (1673; repr., Morgan: Soli Deo Gloria, 2000), 1:184.

3. Philip Kennicott, "Sackler Displaying Cyrus Cylinder, an Artifact with Long History and Many Meanings," Washington Post (March 7, 2013), http://www.washingtonpost.com/entertainment/museums/sackler-displaying-cyrus-cylinder-an-artifact-with-long-history-and-many-meanings/2013/03/07/e6312362-8765-11e2-9d71-f0feafdd1394_story.html.

4. Charles Spurgeon, "The Treasury of David: Psalm 123," The Spurgeon Archive, http://www.spurgeon.org/treasury/ps123.htm.

5. Thomas Watson, The Lord's Prayer (1692; repr., Edinburgh: Banner of Truth, 1999), 31.

6. Calvin, Commentary on the Book of Psalms, 6:5.80.

7. George Swinnock, The Works of George Swinnock, 5 vols. (1868; repr., Edinburgh: Banner of Truth, 1992), 2:122. Italics mine.

8. Jessica Knoblauch, "Dangerous Mercury Spills Still Trouble Schoolchildren," Scientific American (May 5, 2009), http://www.scientificamerican.com/article/mercury-spills-trouble-schoolchildren.

9. Henry, Commentary on the Whole Bible, 716.

## Chapter 5

1. Josh Moody, Journey to Joy: The Psalms of Ascent (Wheaton, IL: Crossway, 2012), 82.

2. Stephen Charnock, Discourses upon the Existence and Attributes of God, 2 vols. (Grand Rapids: Baker, 1990), 2:13.

3. Isaac Watts, "I Sing the Mighty Power of God," 1715.

4. R. C. Sproul, Loved by God (Nashville: Word, 2001), 57.

5. John Stott, The Message of Romans: God's Good News for the World (Downers Grove, IL: InterVarsity, 1994), 255.

## Chapter 6

1. I am indebted to Carl Trueman for these insights. See http://www.mortification ofspin.org/mos/postcards-from-palookaville/coming-soon-to-a-town-near-you#.VFj0uvnF-So.

2. Moody, Journey to Joy, 69.

3. John Owen, The Works of John Owen, 16 vols., ed. W. H. Gould (London, 1850; repr., Edinburgh: Banner of Truth, 1977), 11:263.

4. Paul Tripp, Instruments in the Redeemer's Hands: People in Need of Change Helping People in Need of Change (New Jersey: P&R, 2002), 241.

5. John Piper, Brothers, We Are Not Professionals: A Plea to Pastors for Radical Ministry (Nashville: Broadman & Holman, 2002), 115–16.

6. Henry Smith, as quoted in I. D. E. Thomas, A Puritan Golden Treasury (Edinburgh: Banner of Truth, 2000), 162.

7. Thomas Manton, The Complete Works of Thomas Manton, 22 vols. (Birmingham, AL: Solid Ground Christian Books, 2008), 10:304–5.

## Chapter 7

1. Manton, Works, 19:416.

2. John Blanchard, The Beatitudes for Today (Surrey, UK: Day One Publications, 1999).

3. "What Is the American Dream?," Library of Congress: Teachers: Classroom Materials: Lesson Plans: The American Dream, http://www.loc.gov/teachers/ classroommaterials/lessons/american-dream/students/thedream.html.

4. Henry, Commentary on the Whole Bible, 717.

5. As Don Carson explains, this is a stylistic devise known as inclusion, meaning that everything bracketed between the first and last Beatitudes belongs together. The Sermon on the Mount: An Evangelical Exposition of Matthew 5–7 (Grand Rapids: Baker, 1978), 16.

## Chapter 8

1. Martyn Lloyd-Jones, Studies in the Sermon on the Mount, 2 vols. (Grand Rapids: Eerdmans, 1962), 2:130.

2. John Owen, as quoted in Puritan Golden Treasury, 175.

3. Joachim Neander, "Praise to the Lord, the Almighty," 1680, trans. by Catherine Winkworth, 1863.

4. Wells, No Place for Truth, 170–71.

## Chapter 9

1. Thomas Watson, The Beatitudes: An Exposition of Matthew 5:1–12 (1660; repr., Edinburgh: Banner of Truth, 1994), 25.

2. Matthew Henry, Matthew Henry's Commentary on the Whole Bible (Iowa Falls: World Bible Publishers, n.d.), 3:793.

3. John Flavel, The Works of John Flavel, 6 vols. (London: Banner of Truth, 1968), 3:245.

4. John Bunyan, A Treatise on the Fear of God (Morgan, PA: Soli Deo Gloria, 1999), 29.

5. William Gouge, Of Domesticall Duties: Eight Treatises (London, 1622), 8.

6. The following is adapted from Moody, Journey to Joy, 103–4. Moody, in turn, summarizes insights gleaned from Carl Zimmerman's Family and Civilization (1947), and Edward Gibbon's The Decline and Fall of the Roman Empire (1776–1778).

7. Bunyan, Fear of God, 77.

8. I am indebted to George Swinnock for his insights in Works, 4:508.

9. I am indebted to Chris Brauns, Unpacking Forgiveness: Biblical Answers for Complex Questions and Deep Wounds (Wheaton, IL: Crossway, 2008), 64–73.

## Chapter 10

1. As quoted by William MacDonald in Alone in Majesty: The Attributes of a Holy God (Nashville: Thomas Nelson, 1994), 120–21.

2. Owen, Works, 6:324.

## Chapter 11

1. Owen, Works, 6:334.

2. Thomas Watson, All Things for Good (1663; repr., Edinburgh: Banner of Truth, 1994), 28.

3. John Bunyan, The Miscellaneous Works of John Bunyan, 12 vols., ed. Owen Watkins (Oxford: Clarendon, 1988), 10:111.

4. Owen, Works, 6:360.

5. Owen, Works, 6:396.

6. I am indebted to Timothy Keller for his insightful treatment of this subject in King's Cross: The Story of the World in the Life of Jesus (New York: Penguin, 2011), 98–99.

7. Horatio Spafford, "It is Well with My Soul," 1873.

8. Victor Frankl, Man's Search for Meaning (New York: Washington Square, 1984), 163.

## Chapter 12

1. Thomas Manton, An Exposition of the Epistle of James (London: Banner of Truth), 353.

2. Jonathan Edwards, Charity and Its Fruits: Christian Love as Manifested in the Heart and Life (1852; repr., Edinburgh: Banner of Truth, 1969, 2000), 130.

3. Edwards, Charity and Its Fruits, 133–34.

4. Owen, Works, 9:119.

5. Manton, Works, 21:439.

6. Priscilla Owens, "We Have an Anchor," 1882.

7. I was reminded of this famous poem in Moody, Journey to Joy, 145.

## Chapter 13

1. A. W. Pink, An Exposition of Hebrews (Grand Rapids: Baker, 2004), 887.

2. Swinnock, Works, 2:336–41.

## Chapter 14

1. Stott, Message of Romans, 375.

2. Thomas Watson, as quoted in A Puritan Golden Treasury, 148.

3. Terry Johnson, When Grace Transforms: The Character of Christ's Disciples Put Forward in the Beatitudes (Fearn, Ross-shire: Christian Focus, 2002), 65.

4. William Perkins, A Godly and Learned Exposition upon Christ's Sermon on the Mount, in The Works of William Perkins, 3 vols. (London, 1631), 3:17.

5. Johnson, When Grace Transforms, 115.

6. Pink, Hebrews, 1110.

7. James M. Boice, Romans: The New Humanity (Grand Rapids: Baker, 1995), 1780.

8. Flavel, Works, 5:247.

## Chapter 15

1. I am indebted to George Swinnock for his insights in Works, 4:399–400.

2. John Calvin refers to God's hidden will as his "secret plan," "secret providence," "secret judgments," "incomprehensible plans," and "secret direction." Institutes of the Christian Religion, in The Library of Christian Classics, 2 vols., ed. J. T. McNeill (Philadelphia: Westminster Press, 1960), 1:16.2–9; 1:17.1–2; 1:18.1–4.

A Hope Deferred

ADOPTION AND THE FATHERHOOD OF GOD

J. STEPHEN YUILLE

We use the word adoption very casually today—
we speak of adopting pets, books, and highways.

Yet the word has a far nobler significance.

Adoption is the permanent placement of a child in a
family with all its rights and privileges. God has
forever placed us in his family. He has forever
made us his children. He has forever changed our
legal status. *A Hope Deferred* probes the depths of
this wonderful reality and intertwines these blessings with an account of one family's journey to
international adoption. The result is a valuable
glimpse into the essential relationship between
adoption, affliction, and the fatherhood of God over
his people.

Available in print or eBook

**www.ShepherdPress.com**